DESERT
SOLDIERING

THE GULF IN THE SIXTIES

DEREK
DOWEY

For my lovely Alison

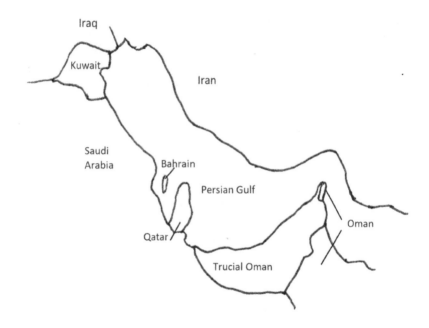

Iraq

Kuwait

Iran

Saudi
Arabia

Bahrain

Persian Gulf

Oman

Qatar

Trucial Oman

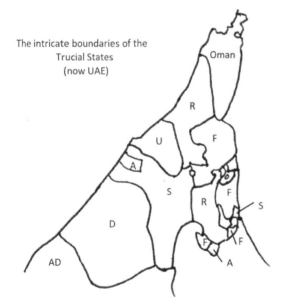

The intricate boundaries of the
Trucial States
(now UAE)

Oman

R

U

A

F

S

R

F

S

D

F

F

AD

A

A	Ajman
AD	Abu Dhabi
D	Dubai
F	Fujairah
R	Ras-al-Khaimah
S	Sharjah
U	Umm-al-Quwain

INTRODUCTION

In 1959, the 1st Battalion The Royal Inniskilling Fusiliers was based out-side Wuppertal, West Germany. It was a good place to be – a fine pre-war barracks surrounded by beautiful countryside. However, most of us were delighted at the news of our next posting – Bahrain and Kenya. First we would take leave in the UK before regrouping in Norton Barracks, Worcester. Then proceed, by troopship, from Southampton to Bahrain – there to drop off two companies – with the main body of the battalion going on to Kenya. Wonderful. I left Wuppertal ahead of the battalion. My task was to see the heavy baggage through customs in UK, and also arrange for some 600 travel warrants to be changed into rail tickets so that the troops could go on leave. So I spent a relaxing and enjoyable week at Harwich. Of course, I had work to do with the customs and rail authorities but I had plenty of free time and was made very welcome in the Royal Pioneer Corps barracks. Eventually the battalion came through and the rail tickets were distributed. I was OIC Troops on a troop train destined for Liverpool with the bulk of the battalion on board. As the only officer travelling, I sat in splendid isolation in my own first-class compartment with one 'pip' on each shoulder and a large notice on the window for all to see: 'OC Troops'. At Liverpool Lime Street Station many of us trans-ferred to military trucks for the journey down to the docks and then em-barked on a cross-channel ferry bound for Belfast. The soldiers headed for the bar whilst I, after dinner, made for my cabin. Fortunately, when I went for breakfast the following morning, there was nobody waiting to present me with a huge bill for a wrecked bar; the boys must have behaved them-selves! As the ship nudged against the Belfast dockside there, as usual, was Dad waiting for me. And Mum had the traditional huge Ulster Fry on the table when we got home to Glengormley, north of Belfast. Dad had recently retired from the Army after 34 years of service (most of it with the Inniskillings).

My leave was grand. There were visits to and from relatives (the Dowey and Dickson tribes), some walking with Dad, a few sports events and lots of good eating. Also, the start of a tradition which was repeated whenever I went home on leave to see Mum and Dad – on an evening selected by Mum, she and I would go greyhound racing at Dunmore Stadium in Belfast. We were invariably lucky and would win enough for the next part of the tradition – a slap-up meal in one of the many Chinese restaurants in town. (Having spent some years in Hong Kong, it always amused us when a young Cantonese waitress asked if we were ready to order – in a broad Belfast accent.) A feature of Army life is that you meet nice people and then move on, possibly never to see them again. The night before I left Belfast to return to the battalion, I attended a party and bumped into a girl who was in my class at Omagh Academy six years before. She had been a lively 'tomboy' at school. I couldn't believe how much she had changed; she was simply beautiful. However, I was off to Bahrain and didn't intend to spend my time pining over a girl who I wouldn't see again for at least a couple of years. So it was a matter of, "Great to see you again," but no exchanging of addresses.

CHAPTER 1

PERSIAN GULF: BAHRAIN AND TRUCIAL OMAN

1961

In those days travel by troopship was normal, with only small drafts occasionally travelling by air. Around ten troopships were in regular operation, five being owned by the Crown and the others remaining the property of shipping companies while on long-term charter. On a cold January afternoon in 1960, I found myself on the dockside at Southampton staring up at the troopship *Devonshire*. I had sailed on her with my parents as a seven-year-old boy when the battalion left India for the last time in August 1947 and headed to Hong Kong. I loved the *Devonshire* and it was great to be back on board. Going to a foreign destination by troopship ('trooping' as it was called) was a great way to travel. To me, it was the _real_ way. You could savour the entire journey and arrive partly acclimatised and feeling great after what was really a damn good holiday. Compare that with a cramped ride in an aeroplane and tumbling out at the other end into a strange climate feeling tired and travel-worn.

The departure of a troopship was a grand event. Crowds would gather on the dockside waving frantically, troops at every vantage point waving back, a band playing, bunting streaming and high excitement all round. It would take a while to clear the harbour with tugs heaving and pushing, but eventually you would be bowling along and the little figures on the dockside would gradually fade from sight. As we picked up speed there

1

was an important matter to attend to – lifeboat drill. Notices in cabins and on troop decks showed where every person needed to muster in case of an emergency. Lifeboat drills were taken very seriously on troopships, and here we were, two hours after departure, doing our first drill. Some six years before, the troopship *Empire Windrush* was carrying troops home after the Korean War when she caught fire and sank off the coast of Algeria. Thanks to efficient lifeboat procedures, all passengers and crew were taken off safely, with the exception of two engineers who were sadly killed by the bursting boiler which caused the fire. The OIC Troops on board the Windrush was Lt Col Bobby Scott of the Inniskillings. He did very well throughout the drama. His two sons Mark and Mickey followed him into the Regiment and we served together.

The main event of the day on a troopship was Ship Captain's Rounds. This was essential; one can imagine the eventual state of a troop deck if no inspections were done during a voyage. It started at around 09.00 and took in virtually every part of the ship. A troop deck might accommodate around fifty men, with bunks stacked two or even three high. Each man had a locker to stow his kit but space was very limited. Some of the lower decks did not have the advantage of portholes for fresh air. Ventilation came down through the pipes but in hot weather a troop deck could be so stifling that many soldiers slept on the open decks. We settled down to the ship's routine – muster parades, troop deck inspections (each subaltern was allotted a troop deck and had to ensure its tidiness for the daily in-spection), some military training, lectures, deck games and great food (alt-hough the troops didn't always agree with that… do they ever?!). We were going overseas to do a job so we needed to prepare for that. Lectures were given about the battalion's two destinations: Bahrain and Kenya. And, on the physical side, there was much weapon training (including shooting at balloons off the stern of the ship), physical training etc. But one of the most enjoyable, and indeed relaxing, things to do on a troopship was to stand at a rail chatting sociably while staring out to sea.

Onboard sports included deck games such as deck quoits, deck 'tennis', deck 'hockey' and tug-o'-war. It's likely a boxing tournament would also take place. Quizzes were conducted over the ship's tannoy system and, depending on the initiative of the passengers, 'horse racing'. A firm favourite of the soldiers was Tombola (aka Housey Housey or Bingo). And several times a week a film would be shown on one of the open decks. Card games were very popular, but the troops were careful to keep their money out of sight so one never knew if they were gambling. Tug-o'-war was a big favourite, certainly for the spectators. As David Twigg reported in an edition of the Inniskillings Annual Newsletter:

"The sergeants challenged the officers to tug-o'-war. This was the greatest cheat ever. On account of the layout of the ship, the rope was passed around the mast with the two teams pulling in parallel on either side of the main deck, but out of sight of each other. The officers accepted the challenge and tugged at the end of their rope but with no movement in it at all. Meanwhile, the sergeants (out of sight on the other side of the deck) had secured their end of the rope to a stanchion and stood around with cool drinks in their hands while the officers tried to pull the ship apart!"

Of course, the troops hooted and roared.

Arrival in port was another great occasion. You found a good viewing point and let the seamen do all the work. Some ports are truly unforgettable. One such is Malta. Some of the passengers were destined for Malta, still a Crown Colony and with a British garrison. We remained there for a day for fuel and victualling. Shore leave was granted, so we wandered around the historic town of Valletta with its relics of two sieges: first, in 1565, when the Maltese and the Knights of St John successfully withstood the assault of the Ottoman forces, and then in WW2 when they held out against the Luftwaffe, the Italian air force and a sea blockade. For their amazing bravery in the latter siege, the island earned the George Cross. (And still, after many years of independence, the island nation bears a George Cross on its flag.) During its British period, Malta was home to the Royal Navy's Mediterranean Fleet. And, sure enough, during our short stay we saw plenty of evidence of that. As we left the harbour our

Regimental Band was drawn up on the foredeck. I was standing on a rail alongside a subaltern of the King's Regiment. He was going out to Kenya to join his regiment. He and I had chatted a few times during the voyage. As we passed the cruiser *HMS Tiger*, our band struck up the old jazz classic 'Hold that Tiger!' The matelots on the Tiger cheered themselves hoarse. My friend turned to me and said:

"That's what I've come to expect of the Inniskillings. I'm enjoying being with your regiment during this trip and, although I'm sure I'll like my own, I wish I had been commissioned into yours."

A generous compliment indeed.

Our second stop was Port Said, at the north end of the Suez Canal, where we tied up on buoys mid-channel. We were there for only a short time while the ship refuelled and took on fresh food. However, there was time for the troops to haggle with the bum-boatmen – they had rowboats stocked mainly with trash but nonetheless seemed to make good trade. If you wanted something you shouted down to them (they all understood some English) and agreed a price; they would then sling up a rope with a basket attached. You put your money in the basket, lowered it and then they would haul up your purchase.

The canal pilot boarded and we were soon away in a south-bound convoy. I had been watching a Clan Line ship tied to buoys a little way ahead of us. It wasn't my old ship the *Clan Macleod*, but I wondered if any of my shipmates were on this one. Sure enough, the third mate from my lovely old ship was there; I could see him on the stern (so that meant he was now second mate) directing the crew as they prepared to join the convoy. He was a great chap and thoroughly deserved promotion. I yelled at him on our way past and he looked across but he couldn't see where the shout had come from amongst the masses crowding the rails. *(However, I visited the radio officer and paid him for a telegram chat when the radio cabin had a quiet period in the Red Sea – that seemed a really high-tech thing to do in those days!)* I had sailed through the canal several times. The last time was in 1958 on the *Macleod*. It has always fascinated me. On the west side, running parallel to the main canal, was another one with fresh water. It was used for irrigating the local fields, and it stank. Thus, it had been christened 'The Sweetwater Canal' by the British. The east side was mainly desert, but in parts it was littered with military debris from the Arab-Israeli wars.

Having reached Port Suez at the end of the canal, we headed down the Red Sea. It was a very good time to be doing this – the January weather was grand. And then to Aden, our refuelling and re-supply port. A few of us took the launch ashore, wandered around the town for a bit (and proved that there was nothing much to do or see) and then headed for the garrison beach. The threat of sharks meant that the beach was enclosed by a shark net. The only other interesting thing about Aden town/harbour was the swarm of bum-boats round the troopship, and the young boys who would dive off them in pursuit of coins tossed into the sea by the passengers. Next port of call, Bahrain.

Salaam Alaikum – Peace be on you.

The Detachment of Inniskillings, consisting of A Company, B Company and a small HQ, disembarked in Bahrain in February 1960 after a relaxing three weeks on board *HMT Devonshire*. She then sailed away to Kenya with the rest of the battalion that is C, Support and HQ Companies plus Battalion HQ; also the detachment of the Queen's Regiment which we were relieving. For us in the Bahrain Detachment, February was the perfect month to arrive in the Persian Gulf as the blistering heat didn't usually start until May. B Company (Major Geoff Cox commanding) was to share a barracks with the RAF at Muharraq Airport. Muharraq was a small island just off Bahrain proper, and was joined by a causeway. The causeway was one of the strategic features which we would have to keep open in the event of disturbances. 'A' Company (Major Peter Bettesworth) and Detachment HQ headed off to *HMS Jufair* – the Royal Navy's shore establishment on the north-east side of the main island. The Detachment Commander, Major Jim Larkin, had already arrived by air with the Advance Party.

Bahrain translates as 'two seas' which is appropriate as it is half-way up the Arabian/Persian Gulf (choose which name you prefer). The island was called Dilmun in ancient times and was an important trading post. Persians and then the Portuguese governed the island before the British made it a protectorate in the 1800s. (*It gained full independence in 1971, some ten years after the Inniskillings were there.*) The ruling Arab family was (and, in 2022, still is) the Al-Khalifa. They were determined to build the island into a financial centre as they realised they would be one of the first countries in the area to run out of oil; the mainstay of the economy. The main problem in the country was religion... surprise, surprise! The majority of Bahrainis were (and still are) Shia Muslims, but the ruling family is Sunni. We were aware on our arrival that the island was a tinderbox with religious differences simmering all the time.

HMS Jufair (the Royal Navy has a tradition of naming shore bases as if they were ships) was a pleasant camp which sat beside a harbour. Jufair was well-planted with trees and had extensive sand sports pitches. The barracks were of the Indian Raj style, with outside verandahs... but with fans and huge noisy, and not very efficient, air-conditioners. The AC in my room at the mess was the size of a car... and sounded like a clapped-out one! As the '*HMS*' suggests, we were really guests of the Royal Navy in our small Army enclave near the front gate. Of course, the sailors were happy for us to do the guard duties on the gate! A couple of miles away was the main town of Manama.

Why were we there? Well, Bahrain was strategically placed among existing and potential oil-producing nations and had a defence treaty with the UK; in addition, there was the inter-Muslim tension. Thus, our role in Bahrain was to 'Keep the Peace'. We also had a more general operational role in the Trucial States and in Oman to the south, both of which had long-standing defence and support treaties with the UK. Our first few days were spent familiarising ourselves with our role and with the island generally. We had briefings, poured over maps and drove around looking at important locations such as the oil company camp, the Sheikh's palace, police stations, power stations, water pumping stations, the causeway to Muharraq etc. The oil company was BAPCO – the Bahrain Petroleum Company. It was based in the centre of the island at a secure compound. In summary, we were on the island to keep the status quo and, in that way, to ensure the security of the oil industry.

Serving with the military in Bahrain would remind an older generation of the Raj days in India. Our weapons, vehicles, equipment and uniforms hadn't changed much from that time. Our parade uniform was a short-sleeved shirt, shorts, belt, saffron stockings with green and buff garter tabs, puttees, boots and, of course, blue caubeens with grey hackles. However, in barracks we usually wore just bush hats, shorts and boots. In keeping with a tradition of the Raj, all officers as soon as they could (which meant immediately) were required to sign the senior British representative's guest book. In the case of Bahrain, the senior man was the Political Representative, Persian Gulf – representative of the Queen. His offices and residence were in our *Jufair Camp* so it was an easy task to stroll down there and sign in. Once your name was in that book you went on the Protocol List... in the case of a second lieutenant, fairly low down on the list but on it you were. If you liked cocktail parties, it was a good list to be on. I hated cocktail parties but had to go along from time to time. On one occasion, I fell into conversation with a Persian who sold carpets; apparently not any old carpets but some of the finest in the Middle East. (I found out later that he was one of the richest men in the region.) Anyway, I mentioned that I had recently been to the suq in Manama to buy a couple of carpets. Somehow, he formed the opinion that I knew a lot about carpets. Fortunately, he was garrulous and hogged the conversation. I hadn't the heart to tell him that my purchases had been two cheap 'felt' rugs to cover the concrete floor of my room.

In the really hot weather (May to October), military training was confined to early mornings and evenings/nights. Field training was somewhat limited, but there was a small desert area in the south which we got to know pretty well. Back in barracks, we practised our Internal Security (IS) drills. In those days the drills were rather formal and hadn't changed much for decades. Our riot control formations were based on platoons consisting of three rifle sections and platoon HQ. When deployed, the riflemen with their NCOs formed a square around the HQ element. The latter comprised commander, sergeant, radio operator and runner. In addition to this, one rifleman was assigned as photographer and another as medical orderly. Civilian assistance comprised a local policeman and a representative from the Magistrate's Office. In the event of a civil disturbance (we never had to deal with one) the platoon would drive out in a couple of trucks, debus and form up in 'square formation'. If our order was to disperse the crowd, the platoon would march towards them in the square formation and halt. This show of force was deemed necessary to confirm that we meant business and that they should clear off. If they didn't, bayonets would be fixed on the rifles and a banner unfurled. The banner (in Arabic and English) would state that the demonstration was illegal and that they must leave. Also, an Arabic speaker (usually the policeman) would announce the same message on a megaphone. If that didn't work, two riflemen (with a couple of others as close support) would trot out with a roll of concertina barbed wire and spread it in front of the platoon to show clearly the line between us and them. Again, the megaphone warning was called out. Depending on the seriousness of the situation, gas masks might be donned and gas grenades thrown to disperse the crowd. If the situation was worsening (looting, burning of cars etc.) it might then be necessary to call out, *"Disperse or we fire!"* – in Arabic and in English. Then a section of riflemen would kneel down and load their rifles. The platoon commander would try to spot a ringleader in the crowd, indicate him to the riflemen but tell them to hold their fire. This gradual escalation was designed to encourage the crowd to disperse. Before actually firing, it would be necessary for the commander and the magistrate's representative to confer and then both to sign a document stating the time and the fact that the situation was now such that a shot would be fired. There were different ways to conceal the identity of the soldier who would fire the killing shot. The usual one was that when the soldiers were seen to be loading their rifles, only one (or perhaps two) would load with a live round and the others would load with 'blanks' – training ammunition which made the sound of a shot but did not contain a projectile. Thus, if the order was given to "Fire" several shots would ring out but only one (or possibly two) could do damage. And the shooter would, of course, be a marksman therefore virtually guaranteed to hit the target. This procedure may appear heavy-handed and also cumbersome to the modern reader, but that was the way it was done for many years, right up to the 1960s. Fortunately, we never had to do it for real in Bahrain.

The 'single' soldiers had very little opportunity to meet girls in Bahrain, although some of them visited the prostitutes in Manama. But most seemed to enjoy their time in the Gulf... we were always busy with Infantry training, sport, exercises and operations. It seemed to me that the biggest morale booster for the Detachment was right there in our little camp. It was the Char Wallah's tent. The Char Wallah (Tea Man) had been an institution in the British Army for centuries starting, of course, in the early days of the Raj in India. Over time, the idea of making tea for the troops had developed into an institution which no unit would want to be without. My earliest memory of a Char Wallah was in Lahore in 1946/47 where the Inniskillings' man was Ahmed Din. He commanded his own private company of men with various skills. Char Wallahs provided a sort of NAAFI canteen with the usual food and beverages like bacon butties, egg banjos, coffee and tea, while also stocking day-to-day things a soldier may need such as boot polish, blanco etc. There would be a cobbler, a hair-dresser and, in particular, a dhobi (laundry). The dhobi wallah collected laundry in the morning and returned it by the evening... uniform spotlessly clean and immaculately pressed (or he would be sacked) for a very reasonable price; and they did it all by hand. *If they were near a river (none in Bahrain), they would go down and thrash the laundry on rocks*! If you were ever in a real panic over an item of uniform (perhaps you had just been told that you were to do an extra Orderly Officer duty due to a misdemeanour), you could opt for the 'flying dhobi'. Your jacket/shorts/trousers would be returned for a higher fee in about two hours! Yes – clean, dry and pressed. Magic. Our Char Wallah in Bahrain was an old rogue called Ghulam Hassan. He operated from a large Army marquee, probably one which had been about to be condemned as useless by the Quartermaster. (*As John Masters explained in one of his Indian Raj books – 'One didn't investigate these things too closely… a Quartermaster's world involved mystery and sorcery, and it was better for normal people to stay out of it'.*) Needless to say, the chances of a fire in the marquee were quite high with various kinds of petrol cookers operating throughout the day and long into the night. One of my tasks, apart from being a platoon commander, was Camp Fire Officer and, of course, I had to inspect the Char Wallah's area regularly with my Fire NCO. We provided Ghulam with sand buckets and fire extinguishers and, fortunately, he took the matter seriously. I usually visited when I was dying for a mug of char and a cheese and onion sandwich… you wouldn't get better in the whole Gulf than in Ghulam's establishment. Traditionally the fire officer and NCO were honoured guests:

"You are no pay me nothing, Lieutenant! I am honoured you are come my tent! Any time you are come you are free!"

Well, I got through quite a lot of cheese and onion sandwiches during my time as fire officer that's for sure. Was this corruption? Absolutely not! This was the reward for a young officer doing his job diligently – or so I claim! And it was the way things worked in the days of Empire – "*Don't accept anything tangible, but edibles are allowed.*"

For each 24-hour period there was an orderly officer at work. His duties were many, but he was aided by an orderly sergeant and a duty corporal. For most of the working day each got on with his normal duties; it was in the evenings and at night that they undertook most of their responsibilities – basically the security, safety, discipline and the administration of the camp. And, of course, being the first officer available in an emergency. A recurring duty was the visit of the orderly officer to the troops' dining hall at mealtimes. One lunchtime I was undertaking this particular duty. My first job was to check the menu and then the evidence set out on the hot plates. It looked good to me – wholesome food with a reasonable set of choices; I wished I could tuck in myself! Then I walked around the tables with the orderly sergeant to check if there were any complaints. (This was the time when an 'old' soldier might try to show off to his younger mates. He might like to let them see how to deal with a very junior officer.) A real 'old' soldier who had been in Burma during World War 2 with my father was sitting with his cronies at a table. A competent soldier, he had had a chequered military career – promotion, demotion, promotion and so on. At this time he was in a demoted period – a fusilier:

"Sir, this food is a disgrace! It's unfit for human consumption." (He had a way with words).

"Tell me exactly what is wrong with it, Fusilier."

All went silent in the dining hall. Our man plays to the crowd.

"The whole lot is just disgusting, Sir."

"I have been here for the past fifteen minutes. I have seen the food being prepared and set out on the serving trays. I have seen soldiers clear their plates with no complaints. You need to tell me what *exactly* is wrong with the food."

"It's totally inedible, Sir."

"Take his name, Orderly Sergeant. Charge him. Frivolous complaint." Shock, horror on the fusilier's face. Silence… but several grinning faces in the dining hall. The young subaltern had sorted out the old soldier.

At an Officers' Mess Meeting I had been appointed Food Member; a form of punishment for being the junior member of the mess. However, it suited me fine – I would have the food I wanted, and I enjoyed going down to the fish and vegetable markets with the cook early in the morning to select what we needed for the day. I love fresh markets. Anyway, one evening a captain and I were the only two for dinner. We sat down opposite each other and had an interesting conversation.

Him:

"What sort of haircut is that? The officers of this mess shouldn't have to look at the ugly sight of your haircut when they sit down for a meal. You're not American, you're a British Army officer and shouldn't have a crew-cut."

Me:

"The weather is very hot. Nonetheless we are still training and playing sport. This is the best haircut for this weather, particularly with the need to shower frequently."

Him:

"It's not appropriate for a British Army officer."

I made no reply but concentrated on my meal.

Him:

"And what sort of food is this on my plate?"

Me:

"It's scampi which I bought this morning when I went to the fish market with the cook. It's delicious. The chips are excellent and the frozen peas are almost as good as fresh peas. A simple but good main course."

Him:

"I don't agree. This is not the sort of food to provide for dinner in an officers' mess."

I got up and walked out. He called out after me:

"No, no! I'm supposed to walk out!"

We encouraged the men to play sports and, of course, joined them. Even in the heat of summer many of us played sports at least six times a week. There were frequent inter-platoon and inter-company competitions. We found it better to play on early mornings or later evenings as it was usually cooler then. Hockey, basketball, cricket and especially soccer were the favourites. But there was also squash, tennis, volleyball, athletics, sea-fishing and even rugby. (I was almost a rugby international for Bahrain against Kuwait, but the promised RAF flight to take us up the Gulf to Kuwait was cancelled.) Hockey was our most successful sport – inter-platoon, inter-company, inter-service, against visiting RN ships and also against local civilian teams. One of the best local teams was from the Indian business community, and two of their number had played for India in the

Olympics. The stickwork of the civilian teams was usually very good, but we were able to counter this with half the team being flyers and the others experienced hard-hitting steady players. My platoon sergeant, 'Johnny-Horse' McFadden wasn't a 'steady'. Anything but. He charged around the field like a runaway horse. The only thing steady about him was his steady stream of yells – which were often difficult to understand but seemed to rattle the opposition. Three Hurley (an Irish game, a sort of wild hockey) players formed our attack – Fusiliers Burns, McDonnell and Ward. These chaps didn't waste time trying to control the ball, they simply hit it first time scoring a lot of goals in the process. At the other end of the pitch, in his goalkeeper's armour, stood Cpl Kevin McFerran. Before a match he would take out his false teeth; he reckoned that yells coming out of a wide-open mouth with only a couple of canines showing helped to unnerve the opposition. It did. And he didn't wait patiently on his line. Oh no, he simply charged out at opposition forwards who had the temerity to enter his goal area. Let's say that teams found it difficult to score against us. Up until our last match we had won around 90% of our games and were level-pegging with the oil company BAPCO as top team. They had a sound mixture of European and Asian talent and beat us as often as we beat them.

Inter-platoon soccer was the most prestigious of the sports. One morning I was discussing the upcoming challenge match against '1 Platoon' with Sergeant 'Johnny Horse' McFadden and Corporal Mason, our platoon football captain. They were going through their agreed team sheet with me. And then the last name – the right-winger.

"That's you, Sir."

"No, no. There are at least two better right-wingers in the platoon than me."

"Yes, you're right. But we want you on the wing. We play better when you're on the pitch with us."

Wow! I played a lot of sport in the Army and also after my Army days. But the finest sporting accolade I ever achieved was on that day in 1960 in Bahrain when I was selected to play on the right wing for 2 Platoon, A Company, 1st Bn The Royal Inniskilling Fusiliers.

There were very few young, single ex-pat ladies in Bahrain. Some young bloods claimed that they enjoyed the company of BOAC hostesses who overnighted at the Speedbird Hotel. That may have been true. And there were a few, a very few, young British nurses at the state hospital. We met them at parties and they sometimes came to watch us play hockey. They were very nice. One in particular was super, but she was engaged and couldn't wait to get back to her beau in the UK. No girlfriends Derek? Unfortunately correct, no girlfriends.

Mo Mitchell was an old fusilier with a chest full of war and campaign medals. He had been an Army boxing champion and was coming to the end of his service. At this time his misdemeanours usually involved drink and late nights. But he was loved by all and protected by the mighty. The soldiers weren't supposed to go to the Navy bar, but one evening he was there; he often was. However, the next morning he couldn't be found. Later, someone passing the cricket nets remarked that it looked as if a hurricane had hit them. Now it so happened that the mouth of the cricket nets faced towards the Navy camp. It seems that Mo, on his way back to his billet, had unwittingly entered the open end of the nets and then, at the batting end, found his way impeded. After taking on the nets single-handedly for some time, he had fallen down through sheer exhaustion and slept the rest of the night away. Anyway, there he was the next morning in a tangle of nets sleeping like a baby… apart from the snoring!

One day the adjutant called me into his office to ask if I fancied a two-week attachment to *HMS Loch Lomond*, a Royal Navy frigate. Well, that would be grand. A squadron of frigates patrolled the Gulf 'Keeping the Peace' but also looking out for smuggling (gold in particular), slave trading from East Africa and piracy. So, off I went, together with one of our pipers. The Navy thought it was great to be piped in and out of ports by a real live Irish piper. After a few days of sailing along the coast of the Trucial States, stopping and searching dhows, we arrived at Doha – the port and capital of Qatar – for a 3-day visit. While we were there we played hockey against Qatar. For once, instead of the green and buff of the Inniskillings, I turned out in navy blue for the match falsely billed as Qatar versus The Royal Navy. Hardly! On the second evening, the ship hosted a party on the quarterdeck for the worthies of Doha (it was a small, undeveloped place in those days, so there weren't that many people to invite). The ship's officers were in their best blues and I was the only one wearing a scarlet jacket. It was grand that the guests kept looking at me. However, I found out why when I went to the toilet: the mirror revealed that my borrowed clip-on bow tie had come adrift on one side and was dangling. Served me right for wearing a clip-on! Anyway, later I was talking to someone who turned out to be the Chief Fire Officer for Qatar. By way of conversation, I mentioned that I was the fire officer for our detachment in Bahrain. This seemed to impress him, although I tried to explain that our fire equipment consisted of buckets of sand and some fire extinguishers. Anyhow, it was arranged that I should visit the fire station the next morning. I could bring one of the ship's officers along and a car would pick us up from the jetty. The following morning we duly went ashore in T-shirts, shorts and sandals. Arriving at the fire station we saw that the fire crews were lined up in the forecourt, so we decided to wait in the car until the inspection was over. We were wrong. The Chief Fire Officer came over to tell us that we were to do the inspecting and that the Arab firemen were in a high state of excitement about it. So we inspected. Dressed in T-shirts, shorts and sandals! Most embarrassing. But the firemen seemed to think it was a great thing to be inspected by an officer from the British Army and one from the Royal Navy.

When I returned to Bahrain, I had to remove my well-loved Inniskilling grenade cap badge (it was Dad's), as the three Irish regiments had lost their individual regimental depots and now had a combined one. Although we retained our individual identities, our cap badge was now a silver harp with the inscription 'North Irish Brigade'.

In those days there were two Omans: 'Muscat and Oman' (now simply Oman) on the east side of the horn of Arabia, and the 'Trucial Oman' (now the United Arab Emirates) on the west side. On return to Bahrain from my trip with the Royal Navy, I was told to pack my operational kit right away as A Company was about to embark with vehicles on an LSL (Landing Ship Logistics). We were to disembark at Dubai in the Trucial Oman. As our ship crept up the creek in Dubai, we noted that, apart from the police station which had two stories, the buildings were single-storey with wind turrets on top. Just a small fishing and trading (including smuggling) port. *How could we have guessed that the tallest building in the world – the Burj Khalifa – would be built there more than 50 years later?* From Dubai we headed for Sharjah airfield, which was shared jointly by the RAF and HQ Trucial Oman Scouts (TOS). The ten-mile drive took us as many hours. Our drivers were unused to coastal driving – the salt flats kept bogging us down. We eventually learned that you had to drive where you could see puddles of saltwater lying on top – that was firm ground.

In Sharjah we met two of our fellow Inniskillings who were on secondment to the TOS: Captains Malcolm Vining and Brian Smith. They were able to brief us about the Trucial States and give advice on desert driving. We needed it because our orders were now revealed – to cordon and search villages in the inland Buraimi Oasis area. It was suspected that they were serving as a transit armoury for the rebels in the mountains over the border in Muscat and Oman. (Weapon smuggling in those days was from Saudi Arabia. The weapons had been obtained in the United States.) So, we set off bogging down in the sand, breaking down and generally making eejits of ourselves. We bumbled along for hours, with me in the last vehicle of the company. It was getting dark when the column stopped suddenly, so I walked up to the leading vehicle to find out what the problem was this time.

"We've lost the column, Sir. There are no tyre tracks."

"When did you last see tyre tracks?"

"Not sure."

"Bloody hell!"

With difficulty, and not too much bogging down, the vehicles were turned around and we headed back the way we had come. It was slow going because it was now night and we couldn't show any lights... the cordon and search operation due to take place at dawn was supposed to be secret. The long and the short of it was that we eventually blundered into the company encampment to find that, for diplomatic reasons, the cordon and search operation had been called off. Phew!

While we were still in the Buraimi area, the officers were invited to a fadl (Arab feast) by Sheikh Zaid; the Sheikh of six of the Buraimi villages. *In the 1950s, Saudi Arabia had laid claim to one of his villages and there was considerable tension for some time until the TOS decided they had had enough of it and chased the Saudis out. Of course, the problem was all about oil. Drilling nearby had indicated large oil reserves.* For the fadl the TOS had offered their squadron outpost of Buraimi Fort as the venue – after all, Zaid had been born there! – and he provided the food. It really was an amazing feast. The main feature was a young camel stuffed with a goat which, in turn, had been stuffed with chickens. When this mountain was well and truly cooked, the chefs set to tearing the meat into pieces, setting them on huge round trays and surrounding the meat with rice. We, as guests, were in the circle surrounding the feast and had first choice, along with Zaid's senior staff who were dressed up in their desert finery and well-accoutred with weapons. My first attempt to get something to eat wasn't successful. It was evening and the hurricane lamps weren't throwing much light. My chunk of meat turned out to be mainly gristle. I was squatting beside John Curtin and asked his advice on how to get rid of it. I could hardly sling it over my shoulder as Sheikh Zaid's 'second eleven' were squatting behind us awaiting their turn to eat – *international incident, slinging pieces of meat at the hosts.*

John whispered:

"Put it back on the tray."

So I made a careful scrutiny of the chunks of meat on the tray, selected a likely target, and then made a lightning strike, dropping the offending piece and picking up a new bit all in one flowing movement. So that was alright. A couple of minutes later I noticed one of the Sheikh's entourage having a lot of trouble with a large piece of chewy gristle – even with the dimmed lighting it looked quite familiar!

(Postscript. Sheikh Zayed's brother, Shakhbut, was the Ruler of Abu Dhabi at this time, 1960. An old-style Bedu, Shakhbut kept the trickle of oil revenues to himself – literally hiding some of the cash under his bed. Even when the oil money became a flood, the people of Abu Dhabi hardly benefitted at all – Shakhbut reckoned the revenues were all his. In August 1966 a Palace Coup occurred, ably supported by the British. Our Buraimi host of 1960, the forward-looking Zaid, took over from his brother and Shakhbut was exiled. After a few years Zaid allowed his brother back and Shakhbut saw out his days in comfort in Buraimi. The enlightened Zaid was a clever and popular ruler and became one of the richest men in the world.)

Now that there was no cordon-and-search operation, each platoon was assigned an area of desert/mountain to patrol, to 'Show the Flag', and to map. The existing maps of the Trucial Oman were very rudimentary so this was a chance to improve them. We patrolled and mapped for a few days, and by the end had set down quite a lot of rudimentary information about the area which might help mapping experts later. I named one feature 'Wadi Curtin' after John Curtin (attached to us from B Company), and he in turn named a hill feature 'Jebel Dowey'. No doubt the real mapmakers soon discarded the names of these early 'explorers'.

At the end of our patrolling and mapping we met up with a squadron of Trucial Oman Scouts consisting of two British officers and the remainder Arabs, mainly desert Bedu. They challenged us to a shooting match. On one side of a wadi they had set up two sets of large biscuit tins filled with sand. There were ten tins in each group. A team of four would represent each side. Peter Bettesworth told me to select three of our other marksmen. Well, we lined up below the ridge beside the TOS team. We were to run up on to the ridge (about a hundred yards away) and then engage the targets which were another hundred yards away on the other side of the wadi. There would be no prior zeroing of the rifles. Ten rounds for each rifleman and the winning team to be the first to knock down all the targets. The rest of our company and the squadron of TOS watched. The

TOS soldiers were in a state of high excitement and already yelling their support – the Desert Men were to take on the British Army.

"Go!"

We trotted up on to the ridge, (you don't race up otherwise you would be breathless when you tried to shoot) then flopped down into the prone position and started shooting – aimed shots, no panic. But what's happening? The TOS supporters were yelling their heads off because some of their biscuit tins had been knocked over... but the Inniskilling tins were all still standing. What the hell!? Anyway, we continued to shoot until our magazines were empty. Couldn't believe it. They had fired off all their ammunition and had four tins down. We had none! Peter Bettesworth:

"What went wrong, Derek?"

"Let's have a look at our targets, Sir."

Our tins were riddled with bullet holes. The rounds had gone straight through the tins without toppling them. We encouraged the TOS to come and look. *Had to maintain the honour of the Regiment!* Mystery solved: we had new 7.62 SLR rifles and the TOS had the old Lee Enfield .303 calibre. The slower speed of the TOS bullets meant that a hit would knock their tins over. The velocity of our bullets took them straight through our tins without toppling them. The TOS looked rather disgruntled about that.

Time to sail back to Bahrain. The boys were glad to be back on board the Royal Navy's LSL. As one of my soldiers said:

"They can keep that desert sand, Sir. There's far too much of it down there. At least in Bahrain we have only one wee desert."

And they were looking forward to the Navy rum ration. On the trip down some of the Old Sweats had lurked in dark recesses and, as the younger soldiers walked away from the rum queue with their mess tins sloshing with rum, they were ambushed by the Sweats and encouraged to hand over their 'tot'. But eagle-eyed NCOs soon put a stop to that:

"Youse are all entitled to one tot only! Youse old crows must stop trying to make the young fellahs hand over theirs."

19

As we sailed we chatted about the Trucial States. I had found the desert and the mountain ranges fascinating. And although we could not converse with the Bedu we met, we found them to be genuinely hard men who had carved out lives for themselves and their families in what seemed at first to be a very hostile territory. Hard as nails but friendly and hospitable. (*I must have caught the 'Desert Bug' as I went back to serve with the Trucial Oman Scouts in '67-'68.*)

Back in Bahrain we were told that our Company Commander, Peter Bettesworth, would be leaving. Peter was a cheerful, quiet man who was easy to work with. Anyway, Peter left soon after he handed over to Major Bill Copinger-Symes. Bill hit us like a hurricane... and didn't seem to think much of us. His many questions included what we did with our platoons outside the training timetable. Well, we organised lots of sports for them. What else? Well, nothing; they needed some free time. Apparently that wasn't good enough. We should run classes to help them pass the various Army Certificates of Education which were required for promotion. So, we took that on as well... and, strangely enough, we were quite successful. At the breakfast table one morning, soon after his arrival, I made some remarks about the new company commander. They weren't complimentary – he seemed to find fault in just about everyone and everything, but surely we weren't that bad? Others at the table held fingers to their mouths indicating "Shut up!" and then pointed to the curtain which separated the dining room from the anteroom. Apparently, Bill had already had his breakfast and was now sitting in the anteroom having a coffee and reading a paper; he had probably heard every word I'd said. So that can't have helped my standing. Anyway, we subalterns worked hard but without enjoying it much while he got us operating in the way he wanted. Came the time when he organised a desert night march in the south of the island. The platoons set off at the same time but on different compass bearings and routes, all to finish on a beach at the southern tip of the island, having covered the same distance and been ambushed by 'enemy' along the way. The long and short of it (and it was long!) was that

20

my platoon reached the destination well inside the planned time, while the other platoons struggled in later.

"Your platoon did well last night, Derek," admitted Bill.

Shock. They were the first words of praise I had heard from him. I strolled along the beach thinking that maybe I was beginning to understand this man. His standards were high and he was going to make sure that his company met them.

Bill usurped me as captain of hockey. Up until then, while wearing the number 7 shirt of the right-winger, I had given myself a roving role on the pitch – turning up where I thought I was needed. Bill wasn't having this and insisted I stay on my wing, "To be there to receive the ball, run with it down the wing, and then whack it into the centre."

Thus, having scored at least a goal a match up to then I didn't score any more. Grumble, grumble.

My platoon (2 Platoon) was good, roughly 50-50 Regular and National Service. Some of the NS men were super (until they got within a few weeks of discharge) and one in particular was outstanding. Mason, a London Irishman, took to Army life like a fish to water and achieved the rank of full corporal within a year – very few NS men in the Infantry managed that. He simply did everything very well, was well-liked and was a great all-round sportsman. Unfortunately, we weren't able to convince him to sign on. He would have made a grand officer. My platoon sergeant was a great character. 'Johnny Horse' McFadden was a very tough Londonderry man who was enthusiastic about everything he did. Opposition players avoided him on the sports pitch due to his all-action 100 mph style of play. And he kept the platoon well disciplined. One morning I was walking with him past the soccer pitch. It was a sand pitch which was rolled regularly. I could see an area with many scuff marks on it whereas the rest of the pitch was smooth. I remarked that it seemed unusual. He explained why. Apparently, his approach to minor breaches of discipline was to inform the miscreant that he had the choice of being on a charge or taking his (Johnny's) punishment. If the choice was the latter then there would be an evening rendezvous out in the gloom of the soccer pitch. At last, I knew why the abrasions on Johnny's knuckles never seemed to heal, and why from time to time fusiliers appeared on Muster Parade with black eyes and split lips claiming that they had fallen over somewhere. Keeping one's charge-sheet clean was important to most soldiers as charges could affect promotion prospects. Thus, they usually opted for Johnny's punishment.

'A' Company was required for another operation on the mainland. This time in Muscat and Oman (now, simply, the Oman) and we were to travel by air. We flew down in Beverleys. These were huge RAF beasts with double-decks and twin booms. They didn't look as if they could fly but they blundered along at low altitude. As we crossed a desert, I swear that on one occasion a herd of frightened camels outpaced us for a few minutes. But Beverleys were great workhorses which could carry vehicles as well as troops. And they had the ability to take-off and land on short, rough landing strips. I was looking out of a porthole as we landed up-country in the Oman at Firq. Actually, I couldn't see anything owing to the sandstorm that these huge planes kick up when landing on a sand strip. (*Overlooking the landing strip was Crown Hill, a feature which a company of the Cameronians had to assault and capture a couple of years before. The rebels – anti-Sultan groups – had installed themselves there.*) We climbed onto trucks which took us past Nizwa, a former stronghold of the rebels, and then a few more miles to the tiny village of Kamah at the foot of the Jebel Akhdar, The Green Mountain. The Akhdar was used as a hide-out by the rebels who were trying to overthrow the Sultan. They waited for arms and mines being smuggled in from Saudi Arabia. Our job was to get up into the mountains, patrol them and make our presence known, but also to set up ambushes in the hope of catching arms smugglers. Frankly, the latter was always going to be unlikely as the 'Bush Telegraph' would have warned the rebels of the arrival of British troops. Anyway, we could at least 'Show the Flag'. The Green Mountain is well-described by an anonymous traveller in the 1830s:

The Jebel Akhdar is something of a geological showpiece. It was apparently formed by a block of limestone, twenty miles across, suddenly thrusting itself up into the world above. This large block had been lurking several thousands of feet deep in the earth. As the central lump forced its way upwards its layers opened out in much the same way as the petals of a flower, until the soaring massif stopped its ascent and the burst limestone strata were left leaning all around it looking like the points of a crown surrounding a mountainous bald pate. These encircling slabs, of a roughly triangular shape, had their apexes at between seven and eight thousand feet, facing inwards and over-looking the flattish top of the Akhdar plateau. The plateau was inhabited, with one fair-sized town and three or four small villages. Water was abundant, the climate mild: the mountain harvests were more Mediterranean than Arabian, barley and grapes and walnuts. The people were ill-mannered, reclusive, and addicted to the wine they made from their grapes.

Yes, the writer travelled there in the 1830s. Surely his description would now (1960) be badly out of date? Not at all. Life in most of Muscat and Oman was still being lived as it had been for hundreds of years.

To get on to the Akhdar plateau from the plains below you either walked or flew. There was a flattish bit of land on top where a skilful pilot could land a small plane; not much good for a company of Inniskillings. Having been driven to the village of Kamah at the base of the mountain, we did what the Infantry was usually required to do... we walked. An Inniskilling officer was doing a short assignment in charge of the small base at Kamah where the best mountain path started. Robin Anderson had 'gone bush' but quickly arranged sufficient donkeys to carry our heavy items – rations, water etc. But we had to supply the donkey handlers from within the company! My batman, Fusilier Hagan volunteered to be one. (Perhaps on the basis that if he could look after and protect an officer, he could do the same for a donkey!) From Kamah it was a foot-slog up a mountain path to a plateau at a height of some 6,500 feet. In some places the path had steps cut into the rock. Apparently, these steps were cut during the Persian time in the Oman (the Persians were there from 500 BC to 600 AD). All the way up, we were aware that the 'adoo' (the rebels) might try a few pot-shots at us. Once we were on top, we all enjoyed the Akhdar, particularly the lovely weather after the heat of the lowlands. The patrolling was strenuous but worth it for the feeling that we were doing something useful and not simply training. Not to mention the wonderful views. On one occasion my platoon was patrolling through a small village of stone houses. From the noise of children chanting, one of the buildings was obviously a school. I asked our guide/interpreter (an Arab corporal in the Sultan's Armed Forces) what the children were learning.

"The Koran."

"What else?"

"Nothing else. Just the Koran."

The self-styled 'Lord of the Mountain' (and chief rebel) was Suleyman bin Hamyar. He had a band of rough bodyguards, and he needed them. He never stayed in a village for long. If he was to stay the night, he would choose one of the village women and tell his henchmen to get the husband away. Then he thrust his well-known walking stick into the eaves of the hut above the entrance and stayed the night there. Nobody would enter while his stick was in the eaves. Well, we didn't catch the scoundrel Suleyman nor anyone else through patrolling and setting up ambushes near paths, but our presence had curtailed the smuggling for a period.

Soon after our return to Bahrain, the Navy took us away again. This time on a four-day trip down the Gulf on an LST (Landing Ship Tank) *HMS Redoubt*. We were to practise assault landings on beaches; the little barren island of Srabu Nuair proved just right. The LST, with its very shallow draft, would run on to a beach, let its assault door down and the Inniskillings would charge off to 'secure' the territory.

"No, that wasn't good enough. We'll do it again."

It took some time before Bill C-S was satisfied with our efforts to storm ashore, fan out, and be ready to take on all-comers. Later another LST *(HMS Parapet)* delivered C Squadron of the 3rd Carbiniers with eight Centurion tanks. The Carbiniers were a super bunch, and we had a great live-firing exercise with them, with the Navy trotting around on this strange stuff – land – as 'enemy'. The tanks were fully closed down but the supporting Infantry platoon commander could talk to the tank commander through the telephone in the rear and indicate imaginary enemy positions (no, the Navy had gone by then). So, with a bunch of Inniskillings hanging on for dear life, we would go into the attack towards unsuspecting rocky pinnacles. Then jump off to allow the Centurions to fire. Blimey! What a racket and what a shower of rocks! With blood-curdling yells we would then attack the blasted rocks and 'mop up'. Great regiment; the 3rd Carbiniers. Sadly no longer in existence.

Time to cool off. From the CSM:

"Youse all deserve a swim in the sea, but before you go in we're going to show you how you can make a raft for all your kit so you can swim with it. Yes, I know there aren't many rivers to swim across in Arabia, but you may have to do it when we go down to Kenya!"

And so, we made our 'rafts'. You spread your waterproof cape on the ground, piled your kit on top, stripped off and put your clothes over the kit before tying the bundle with the toggle ropes we all carried. Launch the 'raft', place personal weapons on top and swim along pushing. And, miraculously, it worked… apart from some dozy fusiliers who hadn't tied the bundle well enough and suffered the consequences.

Then it was time to do Infantry field-firing.

"Derek, see that small jebel to the north-west? There's a wadi behind it. That's your wadi. Fire all your platoon weapons and make sure your fields of fire all point out to sea. Put a couple of sentries up on the high ground to keep others away. Paddy (to Paddy Barnhill) your area is over there to the north-east…" etc, etc.

We had a great time blasting away at various targets, normally large biscuit tins, pieces of flotsam found on the beach or anything else that we could find. Rifles, Bren Guns, Grenades, 2" Mortars and 3.5" Rocket Launchers… all were fired using live ammunition. The boys loved it. And what about the inhabitants of the island throughout all this? Well, there were three of them living in a tent on a sand-spit at one end of the island. The island belonged to one of the Trucial States and these watchmen had been warned earlier that we would be coming to do live firing. So they had got as far away from us as they could. And what were these sentries watching out for? Well, invaders of course. Perhaps Iran or Iraq… but they had their trusty Martini-Henrys to repel them! But no radio contact to tell the mainland what was happening. Ah well, that was the Gulf in 1960.

In late 1960, it was announced that the Inter-Company Athletics meeting would be held just after Christmas. It was to be organised by the athletics officer. Me. What I remember most (apart from arranging almost everything including marking out the track on Christmas morning) was Fusilier Syder throwing the drill grenade. A drill grenade is one that has had the explosive and detonator removed so that it can be used in training. As I couldn't find a javelin, I introduced 'grenade-throwing' to the programme. An average thrower would chuck it 30-40 yards, while a very good thrower would make 50-60. Syder won with a throw of 95 yards. Remarkable.

And then the time came to leave Bahrain. The Advance Party of the new detachment (from the 2nd Scots Guards) was already staying with us, and our detachment had started to thin out with groups flying off to rejoin the battalion in Kenya. Our main hockey rivals (the oil company BAPCO) craftily chose this moment to challenge us to a final match, honours being even at this stage. Six of the First X1 had already left for Kenya (including Bill C-S) so I was hockey captain again. We cobbled a team together and tactics were discussed:

"Let's confuse them. No wild charging around. We'll play stick-work hockey."

After a couple of practice matches, we went down to the oil company in a 3-ton truck to find that they were treating this as a big occasion… this was the day they were to become the undisputed top hockey team in Bahrain. Oil company employees and their families were on the touchline. Our support came from our truck driver and a washer-up from the Char Wallah's tent (an Arab, he nearly always turned up for our matches, knew our names and shouted them out to encourage us). The pitch was super. Perfectly smooth tarmac, with the ball running true and forever. The whistle went and we started to play. And how we played. They didn't know what to do with us. I walked the ball towards their goal and they backed off waiting for the inevitable hard whack to one of the wings. But I kept going and they kept back-pedalling, trying to cover all the options – except one – which was to walk the ball into their 'D' and crack it into the net. That set the tone of our play. This bunch of wild Irishmen had suddenly been transformed into stickwork players. We won 6-1 easing up... and really enjoyed BAPCO's 'celebratory' meal afterwards.

I had enjoyed our year in the Gulf, but we were all looking forward to Kenya. We handed over to the Scots Guards and travelled by the more usual peacetime way for the British Army ever since... no sense of adventure, just get on a passenger aircraft and hope your heavy kit catches up with you later! The troopship days were drawing to a close, so no more pleasant, relaxing journeys to overseas postings and gradually acclimatising as you approached your destination. That's progress? No, it's economics. What a shame.

Fee Aman Allah (Go with God; Farewell).

The officers did not realise that the sergeants had tied their end of the rope to a stanchion!

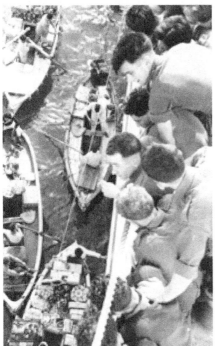

Bumboat men at Port Said

HMT *Devonshire*

January 1960

General speaks to Fusilier Moran. Bill Copinger-Symes on right.

A Company
L to R: Sergeants Lamont, McFadden, Rose, Oliphant,
General Moore, Major Bettesworth, CSM Faulkner

Bahrain Street Security training

Persian Gulf, April 1960

**Oil rig, from the frigate
HMS *Loch Lomond***

**Dhow, which we intercepted,
suspected of gun running**

**Souk in Doha, Quatar
during visit of
HMS *Loch Lomond***

Buraimi Oasis

Having filled jerry cans from a falaj

2 Platoon – Jebel Akhdar 1960

3 Section leaving night ambush

On Patrol Crozier and Hagan (volunteer donkey wallahs)

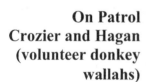

Jebel Akhdar

3 Section on patrol:
Lcpl Robinson, Cpl.
Mohammed (guide)
Donnelly, Cpl Cromie,
Keating, Cahill

Wadi Jizzi, Oman

3 Section + Platoon HQ with Sgt. Orme (TOS)

CHAPTER 2

KUWAIT

1961

And so, from the deserts and jebels of the Gulf to the amazing diversity of Kenya – mountains, forests, jungles, grassland plains, deserts, rivers, lakes and a lovely coastline. Driving in 3-ton trucks from Nairobi airport (altitude 6,000 feet) to our camp in the Rift Valley was a real eye-opener for us 'Desert Wallahs' of 'A Company' who had just arrived from the Persian Gulf. Everything was green or rich brown. There were so many people compared to what we had been used to in the Gulf. Kikuyu women walking along the side of the road with piles of firewood on their heads while singing and sometimes even breaking into a little dance as they went along. Clumps of forest here and there and then down into the Rift Valley to a much more open and agricultural area. Through Naivasha (with the Blue Post Restaurant on the right – just the place to stop for refreshments in days to come) and alongside Lake Naivasha to Gilgil. Gilgil was a dump! It consisted of a crossroads with a few shops and then, in the surrounding area, two or three Army camps. Ours was to the east of the crossroads, at the foot of the Aberdare Mountains. Unfortunately, that year the Gilgil area was a dustbowl due to inadequate rain. If you needed to buy anything in Gilgil you went to the Devonshire Stores. This was run by an Indian family. If they didn't have what you wanted, they would probably get it for you. There were many Indians in Kenya at that time. Not only in the main towns but also in small towns right out in the wilds, and most seemed to be shopkeepers. Our camp was a mixture of low metal buildings used for offices, stores, messes and some for accommodation but most of us lived in tents. Frequent high winds meant that dust covered everything. Later, more metal huts (Twynhams) were erected and we were able to vacate our flapping canvas abodes.

The general feeling in A Company was that we missed the independence of life in the Gulf but that, overall, it was good to be back with the rest of the battalion. Of course, we swapped stories with those who had been in Kenya for a year already. One of their stories concerned the strained relationship between the battalion and the previous commander of our brigade – 24 (Air-Portable) Brigade. He had made a formal visit to check on the battalion's readiness for an emergency fly-out. His inspection was very thorough. With everyone standing out in the baking sun, he ordered that they should unpack their fly-out kit and lay it out for inspection. He then went round slowly and methodically. Right from the start, he was in a foul mood. He even told a senior captain to empty out the contents of his little 'housewife' (repair kit for darning socks etc.) This was getting a bit too much for the Skins and the resentment was building up. Eventually he came to a real old sweat, one with World War 2 service. The soldier's water bottle was attached to his belt. The brigadier tapped the water bottle with his cane:

"What do you keep in there, soldier?"

In a voice loud enough for everyone on parade to hear, the fusilier replied:

"Me fxxxing greatcoat, Sah!"

The shocked brigadier left the barracks very shortly afterwards. No, the fusilier wasn't reprimanded for his remark. He was a hero!

We were continuously at short notice to fly out to troubled spots in Africa and the Middle East. In June 1961, Kuwait gained full independence, having had protective treaties with Britain for many years. Colonel Qasim, the president of Iraq, seemed to think this was his chance. He claimed Kuwait saying that it had been part of the Ottoman Empire and thus was now subject to Iraqi sovereignty. Qasim wanted the Kuwait oil fields. The Kuwaitis called for help and so our formation in Kenya – 24 Brigade – made ready to go to their aid if need be. Apart from making final preparations, nothing significant happened in the battalion for a few days until about 02.00 hours on 30th June. I was orderly officer that night for our camp in Gilgil. A call came through from Brigade HQ to say that the battalion was to fly out from Nairobi Airport to Kuwait within 24 hours. 'Operation Vantage' was rolling. I telephoned the CO in his quarters. He thanked me for the message and said:

"Fine, Derek. We're ready for it, so no need to spread the news until Reveille at 06.00. Let everyone continue with their sleep. I'll be in my office at 06.00 and you can bring me any further messages from Brigade then." Cool, calm and collected Peter Slane…

So the next day the battalion headed for Nairobi Airport. First away was the Advance Recce Party, followed by the Advance Party itself and then the rest of us. Each planeload was referred to as a 'chalk'. My platoon flew out as Chalk 22, i.e., the 22nd aircraft to fly out. But we didn't fly directly to Kuwait for two reasons: there were diplomatic moves going on, and also our planes needed to refuel en route. So the various chalks headed for Bahrain, Sharjah, Masirah (an island off the coast of the Oman) or Aden. Mine landed at the latter and we were whisked off in trucks to a tented Transit Camp for the night. Then back to the airport and away in a Canadair of the Royal Rhodesian Air Force.

(*This was 1961. Thirty-seven years earlier, in 1924, a platoon of Inniskillings had been the first to be air-lifted in a conflict area. That was also in the Middle East – Iraq.*)

My batman at this time was a smashing little man from Belfast, Fusilier Hagan. He was as hard as nails and had been a stoker on Kelly's coal boats around the UK coast. He had a calm, unruffled temperament and could work and march forever. Hagan had been with me for nearly two years and, if there was one thing he knew about me, it was that I could drink tea anywhere and at any time. Alas, there was no galley on our plane to brew up hot drinks. But we had been issued with 24-hour food packs before take-off so we tucked into them. And then, as the plane flew on towards Kuwait, Hagan appeared,

"A mouthful of tay, Sir," in a mess tin.

"Thanks, Hagan. Just the job." (*Pause*)

"Wait a minute! Where did you get this? There are no cooking facilities on this plane."

"Right enough, Sir. I brewed up on my hexamine cooker in the toilet."

"Hagan! (*in a whisper*) You could have set fire to the plane!"

Luckily the crew hadn't noticed this transaction and I sat back and enjoyed my 'mouthful of tay'.

It was the middle of the night, most of us were dozing and then:

"We'll be landing at Kuwait Airport in thirty minutes."

The pilot warned me that although he had permission to land, he didn't know the exact situation on the ground. We made ready to evacuate the aircraft quickly and to spread out around it defensively. We landed, taxied and stopped. The exit door flew open and the emergency steps went down. I rattled down them to be greeted by an English voice:

"What unit?"

"2 Platoon, A Company, The Inniskillings."

"So you must be your battalion Advance Party. You're the first of your lot."

Well, we weren't the Advance Party, we were Chalk 22. We found out later that planes destined for Kuwait had broken down or been delayed all around the Arabian Peninsula. Apart from the Advance Recce Party, 2 Platoon were the first Inniskillings to touch down in Kuwait. The airport had been secured by other British troops, so we headed for the terminal buildings, which were still in a state of construction. One corridor was relatively clean, and we lay down to rest, if not to sleep. I don't think anyone actually slept because of the problem with fiberglass hairs. The prefabricated walls had been in-filled with fiberglass, and there was still a lot of evidence of it around; much of it got into our clothes and itched mightily. Difficult to forget that night. The next day the battalion regrouped at the Kuwait Technical College. Wonder of wonders (at that time)… the lights in the college came on automatically at dusk and went out at dawn. 2 Platoon found a fountain in the grounds. The pool was about four meters across and four feet deep. It held almost the whole platoon standing up. So that was fine, except the rest of the battalion were soon alerted to it. Within a couple of hours it was best avoided; it had turned a sickly green and smelt.

Then on the night of Friday 6/7 July, the battalion abandoned the luxury of lights coming on at dusk (along with the stagnant pool) and headed off to our operational position on the Mutlah Ridge, north of Kuwait City. The ridge rises to about 400 feet and runs north-east and south-west, with the main Kuwait-Iraq road bisecting it. Forty-two Commando Royal Marines had landed from HMS Victorious a few days earlier and we took over from them on the ridge. I usually defend the Royal Marines against any criticism. However, on inspecting the defensive position handed over to me, I was not impressed. We had been told that we would be taking over an entrenched defensive position on the extreme right of the Brigade position. Was it entrenched? No. The Marines had set up sand-bagged emplacements rather than digging in. And they had chosen fields of fire, which puzzled us. (Remember, we were Bill Copinger-Symes' boys and we knew about defensive positions.) So we set to work. Six weeks later, when we left, the position was finished. Why so long? Well, we had flown in with air-portable entrenching tools – shovels and picks – which lasted for about an hour of hacking and digging on the rocks of the Mutlah Ridge. The ground was so hard that we called for support from the Pioneer Platoon. Sergeant Carlin sent along some of his boys to blast into the rock. We had already laboriously cut out the shapes of trenches but weren't making much headway, so they set explosive charges in one.

"Everybody take cover!"

Bang!!

On inspection the shell scrape trench for two soldiers was now about 15 meters in diameter. But it was still less than a foot deep; the charge had simply shattered the rock sideways and had not made any real depth. So that was that.

"It's you, me and shovels and picks, lads."

Virtually all our entrenching tools had to be replaced every day until, at last, we were sent heavy-duty tools. Then we started to make some headway.

Fortunately, in Platoon HQ we had the amazing Hagan – my trench-digger exceptionnelle. He simply laid into the rock. Hour after hour he worked away, interspersed with a swig of water from time to time. And, surprise surprise, our HQ trench was the first to be completed. I made sure that I didn't extol Hagan in Bill Copinger-Symes' presence, as he would probably have pinched him for Company HQ. Bill was never satisfied; he required us to keep improving our handiwork. (In retrospect, he was probably simply ensuring that we always had plenty to do.)

2 Platoon's rest area was in a gully behind the trenches. Several desert camouflage nets had been stretched over it and we all (apart from the sentries) spent the first night under it. The desert can get cold at night and there can even be dew, so it's best to be under some sort of cover. Anyway, we were all under it, and that was not a good idea. Neither Sergeant McLaughlin, the platoon sergeant, nor I really wanted to be right alongside the fusiliers, and nor did they want us there. The next day the two of us moved to a small gully about 20 meters away and, with the addition of a camouflage net, set up our own small rest area. As rest areas go, it was one of the better ones. Our good friend Sgt Rose MM of 1 Platoon had given us a camp bed each. These were very scarce on the ridge as they weren't normal issue items. However, Rose was an experienced and wise soldier and a consummate scrounger! I didn't ask him where he got the camp beds from (that was not the sort of thing to ask Sgt Rose) but I heard later that he apparently picked up four in a storage area as we passed through Kuwait Airport claiming they were needed urgently for 'heat exhaustion cases'. Rose himself, Paddy Ryall his platoon commander, McLaughlin and I were the lucky ones to have camp beds. Paddy had a

private hideaway ('The Shebeen') in a wee gully behind his platoon position. I used to visit for a chat, a mug of char or a fruit drink – so it wasn't really a shebeen at all, was it?

We craved water. This was July and August in Kuwait and the temperature went up as high as 50C/140F. There was no shade apart from under the desert camouflage nets in the rest areas and the kitchen. We sweated when we were working; we sweated standing still. The medical services had instructed that we should have a liquid intake of 32 pints each a day. What?! 4 gallons! That was about a jerry-can of water a day for each man. Unbelievable? No, we needed it. We each had a couple of canvas water containers (chagalls, Arabic word). Evaporation from the outer skin of the chagalls helped to cool the water and we drank frequently from them. Each platoon had a jerry-can depot and there was always a soldier or two going down to fill his chagalls there. In A Company, we had learnt how to deal with the excessive heat from our year in the Persian Gulf and, as a result, we had no cases of heat exhaustion. Infact, I believe that the battalion had only one case during our time on the Ridge. Apparently, a flanking battalion had around a hundred heat exhaustion cases during that time. When we were working there was simply no shade. Working dress was PT shorts, boots with socks rolled down and a bush hat. Those with fair skin wore shirts. To avoid working in the worst heat of the day the battalion adopted a set routine. It was something like this:

03.30	Stand To
04.00-10.00	Work (with breakfast in relays)
10.00-16.00	Rest (lunch in relays)
16.00-19.30	Work (supper in relays)
19.30	Stand To
20.00-21.00	Admin
21.00-03.30	Rest and sleep, apart from those on sentry duty

It was very tiring indeed. And there was plenty of work for the officers and NCOs during the so-called 'Rest' and 'Admin' periods.

To give us a change from the routine and conditions on the ridge, Battalion HQ devised a system which attempted to allow everyone three short breaks during our time there. I did as much sleeping as I could on trips which were –

- Overnight on HMS Victorious a few miles out to sea. This old girl had seen service in the Pacific during World War 2. She carried Sea Vixen aircraft and her radar had a range of 270 kms, a welcome addition to the military force. For us she offered a change of scenery and very good food – just what was needed. But where to sleep? I was shown a pokey cabin in the depths of the carrier. It was sweltering hot in there so I opted for the open deck, and that was great. But not before night-time flying was over. I was taken up onto the bridge to see the Sea Vixens taking off and landing. What a racket! Especially when being catapulted off. But the real drama was as they came in to land on the carrier. You saw the wing lights of the incoming jet rocking from side to side, and you were sure he wouldn't make it. But down he would come, land and be caught by the retaining lines.

- Later, when it was my turn again for a rest trip, I caught a special leave bus on the road near Battalion HQ. We headed for the Kuwait Oil Company installation at Ahmadi on the coast south-west of Kuwait City. A large group of expatriate oil company staff and their families met us at one of their recreation centres. They were really hospitable:

"We'll take two of you for a drive around Kuwait City," or

"Anyone like to spend the afternoon at the pool? We'll have lunch there." And then someone said:

"We've got T-Bone steaks for lunch at home and would like two of you to share them with us."

John Curtin (B Company) and I signed up immediately. Our American hosts entertained us royally. After lunch the offer was:

"Anyone for the swimming pool?" John was all for it. But not me:

"Do you have an air-conditioned room where I could lie down for a few hours?"

43

Certainly they had. So while the others headed for the pool, I lay down on clean sheets in a cool room. Bliss. All too soon, it was time to catch the bus back to the Ridge.

- My final trip away from the Ridge was to the Rest and Recuperation (R&R) tented camp which administrative troops had set up on the seashore at Shaiba, not far from the oil company. We went there in bus loads for 24 hours. There wasn't much to do, but that suited us fine. We just wanted to sit/lie around with a drink in the shade and eat from time to time. It was a good place but we had a shock at 06.00 when pop music blared out over the camp system. We all shouted:

"Shut up! We want to sleep!"

And some of us tramped off to the camp office demanding immediate silence. Then back to bed.

When I got back from my night at the R&R Centre, I found there had been a drama in my platoon position. It concerned the Kuwait Army anti-tank gun section which we had been allocated to help guard the right flank of the battalion. One could hardly call them a professional outfit. They didn't want to dig in and were in danger of being a very obvious target, so we had to get to work on camouflage netting to conceal them. Anyway, it seems that while I had been away, they had got their hands on some beer and became roaring drunk. This was bad enough, but then they thought it would be a good idea to start firing their 120mm MOBAT anti-tank gun up the road at the Iraqis. They were dissuaded and, by the time I got back, they had been removed... permanently! That suited us fine.

At around 15.00 on a stinking hot afternoon, Sgt McLaughlin and I were trying to rest on our camp beds in our little gully when I thought I heard the World War 2 song 'Lily Marlene'. This was long before the days when nearly every soldier had his own music via iPod/transistor etc. I heard:

"Underneath the lamplight, by the barrack gate,
Darling I remember the way you used to wait,
My Lily of the Lamplight, my own Lily Marlene."

I sat up:

"Sergeant McLaughlin, tell me that I'm not going crackers in this heat. Please assure me that you too can hear 'Lily Marlene'… please."

"Sir," he said. "Thank God you can hear it too!"

So we clambered up onto the Ridge and found our sentries buying ice lollies from a Mr Frosty ice cream van… which was playing 'Lily Marlene'.

"Well you lot, thank you for forgetting to tell us about this."

"We were just coming to get you Sir… after we got our ice lollies."

So there it was. A Mr Frosty van out in the desert. A very cheerful Royal Military Police Corporal leaned out of his window to welcome us. Apparently, he had persuaded someone in Kuwait City to hire him a Mr Frosty van on his days off. He would load it up and then set off for the Mutlah Ridge to sell his cargo. He sold everything at cost price and so made a loss because of the hiring fee and his petrol.

"Thought the boys might appreciate it, Sir."

Indeed they did. He should have got a medal.

During 24 Brigade's time in Kuwait I heard of only two fatalities, both in the RAF. One died in a swimming pool accident. The other death occurred much closer to our position; much, much closer. It happened on a windy, dusty day. Not all days in Kuwait were clear and blazing hot. Quite often it was very humid with poor visibility. At other times strong winds picked up the dust and flung it around. On such a day an RAF Hawker Hunter jet fighter was patrolling in front of the Brigade position. This was normal routine for the Hunters. The jet was whizzing backwards and forwards to our front but we only got glimpses through the swirling dust. Anyway, we were digging away and shouting at the plane to push off and leave us in peace (Hawkers made a terrific racket) when there was a sudden silence, followed shortly by a terrific explosion and then another. We could just make out smoke and flames about 200 metres away. We raced across but quickly established that nothing could be done for the pilot; there were body parts strewn around. The inquiry eventually confirmed that the plane had been too low and that the pilot probably realised that and yanked the controls too hard to gain height. The engine cut out and the plane flipped over so that it hit the ground going backwards (first explosion) upside down, bounced, and hit the ground again (second explosion). Just as well that his flight line was slightly away from our position.

The Iraq/Kuwait crisis petered out and Qasim withdrew his threat of invasion. Just in case he changed his mind, the battalion flew down to Bahrain and stayed there for a few weeks so they were close by for a return trip if necessary. In my case, I returned to Kenya and then took another flight to the UK, as I was due to attend two courses – the Platoon Weapons and the Platoon Commanders courses.

Had the British Forces gained anything from the Kuwait deployment? Oh yes: we all, from top to bottom, learnt a lot about being deployed far from our bases. And we had learnt how to live and operate in extreme heat. The Sheikh of Kuwait wanted to reward us all with a campaign medal, but the spoil-sport British Government declined. Of course, we, as young men, were disappointed; we wanted a bit more colour on our jackets.

In the Army, you didn't usually stay long at one appointment or in one place. My posting order came through. I was to be a training subaltern at the North Irish Brigade Depot in Northern Ireland. Well, that should be alright for a while. It should be fun taking on groups of raw recruits and trying to turn them into soldiers in sixteen weeks. Also, I would be able to see my parents frequently... and a certain young lady called Elizabeth. As I boarded the plane for the UK, I reflected on the great time I'd had in Kenya and the interesting one in Kuwait! I would hate to have missed them.

After my time in Northern Ireland I rejoined the battalion in Gravesend, Kent. Just as I was settling in, I was sent away on a six-week anti-tank and mortar course at Netheravon in Wiltshire. With two days to go before the end of the course, there was a knock on my door:

"We've had a message from your battalion. You are to leave the course and return to Gravesend as soon as possible."

"But I can't. There is the last day of training and then the course wash-up."

"Sir, we were told you must return to unit as soon as possible."

Bob Boulton of the Skins was on another course at Netheravon, so he and I crammed into his minivan with all our kit and headed for Gravesend.

The battalion flew into Nicosia airport on February 21 and 22, 1964 to help calm trouble between Greek and Turkish Cypriots, and didn't return to Gravesend until October.

Then, in late 1965, we were posted to Berlin for a second time; having been there in '57-'59. I took over as adjutant from Ronnie McCrum in January 1966. As staff officer to the commanding officer, I knew I had to distance myself from my friends and take on a different persona. This metamorphosis has been described well by John Masters of the Gurkhas in his book 'Bugles and a Tiger':

'There are many ways of being a good adjutant, but several factors are common to them all, and the first three are:
- one must lose all sense of humour
- all sense of proportion
- all desire to win or keep friends.'

2 Platoon 'A' Company
Mutlaa Ridge
Kuwait
1961

**Fusilier McLaughlin
Machine Gunner**

**Sgt McLaughlin
ready for anything**

**Company water point.
A thirsty camel visits us**

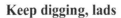

Keep digging, lads

Nairobi Airport - bound for Kuwait SgtKelly, RSM Dick Rafferty

The General points North
Alan Main confirms Iraq is that way. Peter Slane on left.

CHAPTER 3

TRUCIAL OMAN SCOUTS

1967-68

In 1967 it was time to leave the battalion in Berlin. It was certainly a wrench to go... although I knew that most of the junior officers were happy to see me leave. (Nobody likes adjutants much!) The battalion was the heart of the Inniskillings now that we no longer had our own depot back in Ireland. But it was time to move on; and I was certainly looking forward to a tour of duty with the Trucial Oman Scouts (TOS) in the Persian Gulf. First, I had to attend a Colloquial Arabic course at the Royal Army Educational Corps Training School at Beaconsfield, Buckinghamshire.

The Arabic course was intensive but very well-run. Some instructors were from the Educational Corps, but others were Arab civilians. Our main problem was trying to master the sounds of Arabic; the intonation skills of our Arab instructors were needed for that. We were a mixed all-ranks group but most were officers. Just before the first lesson, three individuals appeared in the doorway. Medium height, fit-looking, quite scrawny, confident, no badges of rank. *I know who you chaps are.* Yes, they were SAS. And they were well-prepared. The SAS had insisted they had a working vocabulary of 2,000 Arabic words before they would let them join the course. Although they still had a lot of work to do on pronunciation and grammar, their vocabulary base was of great benefit to them. Most of us made good progress and we were encouraged to converse in Arabic as much as possible... on coffee breaks, in the mess etc.

Six Inniskillings had served with the TOS before me – David Stewart, John Flood, Malcolm Vining, Brian Smith, Peter Kirwan and John Emerson-Baker.

The plane touched down in Bahrain late one night. When the air transport staff found that my smallpox certificate had lapsed, I had a quick vaccination and then an onward flight south to RAF Sharjah arriving at 04.00 hours. A TOS Land Rover bore me away at breakneck speed to the Scouts' new HQ a couple of miles north of Sharjah town. The barracks were called 'Muaskar al Murqaab' – Watchtower Camp – and the entrance was in the style of a Beau Geste fort. My orderly was waiting and lugged my kit into my room. He was a Baluch from the Pakistan/Iran border. His name was Mir Abdullah.

"I'll wake you with tea, Rais Sahib." ('Rais' meant captain.)

And so he did. After a bleary shave, I made my way across to the mess. A few officers were sitting round the dining table. They were concentrating on putting away large amounts of food, but were welcoming enough and suggested I tuck into the food on the sideboard. There was an awful lot of it. Was this lunch? Had I slept through breakfast? Some people were supping soup. An inspection of the sideboard revealed mounds of sausages, bacon, mushrooms, kidneys, beans and fried bread. And eggs to order. Various sorts of sliced fruit, fruit juice, toast, coffee, tea, jam, honey and marmalade. Oh, and there was kedgeree. The soup, by the way, was mulligatawny. Very Raj. So this was breakfast – TOS-style. Fine. I could see that I wouldn't starve.

After breakfast, Mir led me down to the camp tailor to be measured for my uniform. Normal camp uniform was heavy-duty sandals (black), khaki slacks, grey/blue shirt worn outside the trousers, red stable belt, red lanyard, red/white warrior shemagh (headdress), black agul (black twisted rope headpiece to hold the shemagh in place), TOS badges on epaulettes and agul and, of course, badges of rank. Then down to the HQ block to be welcomed by COMTOS (Commander, TOS) who was usually referred to as Al Qaid (The Commander). This was Colonel Pat Ives (late 17th/21st Lancers), a delightful man. (He and his deputy were the only

British officers who were permitted to have their wives with them in the Trucial States.) The Wilson/Falkender Labour Government had recently assured the Trucial Sheikhs that the UK was still very much committed to them and their protection. So Al Quaid in turn assured me that the TOS would be in existence for a long time to come, although it would be gradually Arabised. Already some Arab Officers had been through Officer Cadet School in the UK.

Then there were briefings to attend. The Force was jointly funded by the MOD and the Foreign Office; thus we had a lot to do with the British Political Agent in Dubai, but less with his senior – the Political Resident, Persian Gulf – in Bahrain. After the briefings there were many people to meet in departments around the camp. Finally:

"You will be heading out tomorrow on your induction trip to visit the squadron camps out in the deserts and mountains. You'll have your orderly and a driver. They know the itinerary and it will take you a week. For the first day they will speak English with you. After that, you and they will speak only Arabic. Now this is important – although you will be spending some time with the two British officers at each of the squadron locations to find out what their roles are, you mustn't stay in the camps overnight. All of this is to expose you to as much Jaysh (Army) Arabic as possible. You'll need food for the three of you. Take rations from the QM but you'll probably want to buy some extras – your orderly knows the form. Remember, you have to camp out in the desert every night. Practise your Arabic at every opportunity."

And that's the way it was. The three of us: Mir Abdullah, Juma Saif (our excellent driver) and me, set off in my Land Rover – No.8 was allocated to the Staff Captain. The registration plate simply showed the TOS badge and the number 8. We camped that first night in the desert on our way westwards to Mirfa – the most distant of our camps in the state of Abu Dhabi. 185 miles of generally lousy tracks. Many of the tracks were rutted and had corrugations, but driving on sabhkat was good. Sabhkat is salt-watered sand near the coast and, after many vehicles have compacted it,

52

it is as smooth as glass. In areas where saltwater lay, the drill was to drive on the wet bits but stay off what looked like dry patches. Why? Because where it looked dry was actually swamp and you would bog in. Complicated? Yes. A bit Irish really. On that first evening, we were still quite a few miles short of Mirfa, so we camped out in the desert away from the sabkhat. No tent, just tent walls as protection from the wind; it would get quite cold in the desert at night.

When I woke up in the morning, my orderly, Mir Abdullah was brewing tea.

"Well done, Mir. I'll have some of that, please." He ignored me.

"Hey, Mir. A big mug of tea, please." No reaction.

Then I remembered… no English after the first day. And so I had to struggle with Arabic for the next six days. Otherwise no tea or food and I would be ignored. We set off again after breakfast. I had a rudimentary map and instructed the driver to:

"Go left on that track up ahead." He drove straight on.

"No! Left! Left! You've missed it!" And then I remembered again – tell him in Arabic! Gradually I was able to actually use what I had learnt on the excellent 6-week Arabic colloquial course back in the UK. And I added many local Jaysh (Army) Arabic words: a three-ton truck was a 'Betfort' (you guessed it), 'girbox' meant – no, not a gearbox but a four-wheel-drive Land Rover, and so on. And you used simplified Arabic grammar to hold the nouns together. Jaysh Arabic achieved communication, and so was an outstanding success.

Mirfa camp was by a rocky seashore and was a real dump, mainly a collection of tents and marquees with some small metal cabins for the officers. The only memorable thing about Mirfa was the officers' toilet. It was a canvas and wood structure sited on the rocky shore – a hygienic idea, with the tide doing its stuff. At the entrance there was a flagpole and you hoisted the red flag. This made sense as it meant that someone who was about to plod the 100 metres out in the heat would first check if it was engaged and wait for the all clear, i.e., no flag. At this time, the resident squadron was under the command of a TOS legend, Major Ken Wilson. Ken was a hard, wee Scot who had spent a short time with the Royal Scots as a subaltern but then jumped at the chance of serving with the TOS. He had been with the Scouts ever since. Ken's squadron was made up of Dhofaris from the south of the Sultanate of Oman. They spoke their own Arab dialect and Ken was the only British officer in the force who could speak it. Dhofaris were hard hillmen. They were most effective when isolated from the rest of the squadrons, as they tended to pick fights with the mainly desert Arabs in the other squadrons. Mirfa was as good a place as any to isolate them, although they did rotate to the other camps – after the previous residents had left! Strategically, the camp was well-placed being quite close to the borders of Saudi Arabia and Qatar. Regrettably, it was along this barren coast that unscrupulous Hajj agents on pilgrim ships would sometimes bring their boats close to shore, drop off naive pilgrims, point vaguely inland and tell them that they would reach Mecca after just a short walk – when in reality it was hundreds of miles away. Then the boat would sail away leaving the pilgrims to their likely gruesome plight. TOS patrols would sometimes come across them. Usually dead.

We left Mirfa without any regrets and continued our Trucial States safari. Next stop Buraimi. Well, not quite the next stop. The terrain was so boring that we relieved the tedium by stopping for a brew-up whenever we felt like it, which was often. The only problem with stopping was that out of the seemingly endless and empty desert, a couple or three Bedu would miraculously appear, squat down at a respectful distance and wait to be invited to join us. They would give us local news and, in return, would scrounge whatever they could. After several of these encounters, we started to worry about our rations, so all we gave visitors thereafter was a cup of tea and a few biscuits each – still conforming to Arab hospitality to travellers.

Our usual routine was to set off early after breakfast, have lunch out in the desert or in one of our outposts – if it was close – then drive on until around 16.30 to make camp. On our travels we would stop at certain important villages (Mir and Juma knew which ones... or else they had relatives there) to meet the head Sheikh. Of course, as soon as the villagers saw that the Sheikh had visitors they came piling into his mud/palm-frond hut. Everyone sat around silently clutching their rifles and wearing waist-belt khanjas (knives). The conversation with the Sheikh (in Arabic, of course) would go something like this:

Sheikh: "As-salaamu aleikum." (Peace be with you.)

Visitor: "Wa aleikum as-salaamu." (And peace to you also.)

Sheikh: "How are you?" (Kayfa haaluk.)

Visitor: "Good, and you?" (Ana bekhair, shukran etc.)

Sheikh: "Fine. How's everything?"

Visitor: "Excellent. And with you?"

Sheikh: "Couldn't be better." (All in Arabic).

Then silence.

The Sheikh's coffee bearer would appear bearing a large coffee pot while managing to juggle tiny coffee cups in the other hand. He would go round pouring coffee, first for the visitor, then for the Sheikh and then for all the others. Pour with the left hand, proffer cups with the right, no sugar, no milk. When necessary, he would scuttle off to replenish the pot and then circle with it again. Traditionally, you accepted two refills but the next time he came round you would waggle your cup and he would take it off you. You might well feel relieved about that, as the coffee was sometimes pretty awful. If food/fruit (tinned fruit was a big favourite) was available, the visitor would be offered it first. However, he should refuse it and direct the bearer to someone else. But he in turn would refuse and direct the bearer back to you. So eventually you had to eat first, then everyone else could. After that the Arabic would continue:

Sheikh: "How's everything?"

Visitor: "Everything's fine. And for you?"

Sheikh: "Everything is excellent."

This would go on for some time. Eventually the truth would come out: things weren't all that good.

Sheikh: "Those villagers in xxxxx (the neighbouring state) have been giv-ing us trouble as usual, including trying to steal our best camels. You need to send a patrol up there and warn them to behave themselves." (Mir was my translator.)

And then other problems would come pouring out: water, sick children, bad date harvest etc. I would note them down without promising anything and would pass them on at the next squadron camp.

Eventually Buraimi. The name was given to the general oasis area right out in the desert, almost due east of Abu Dhabi town. There were actually several villages clustered together. Some belonged to the Sultanate of Oman and others to Abu Dhabi; this was where their borders met. Saudi Arabia believed that they owned one of the villages, but the others knew that they didn't. This mixture of territories had led to many problems over the years and was one of the reasons for the formation in 1951 of a military force which eventually became the TOS. Most of the problems revolved around oil exploration in the area, and also the smuggling of arms from Saudi Arabia to the rebels of the Sultanate of Oman. The Saudis obtained these arms from the US. Oh yes, the US didn't like the influence of the British in the area. The US wanted the oil. The TOS Squadron camp in Buraimi was in a fort – Fort Jahili. It looked like something out of the film 'Beau Geste'. The officers' mess was in a large circular tower, and the troops' barracks were in crenellated white-washed buildings which would have formed a fine backdrop for the Gary Cooper film about the French Foreign Legion. The whole thing was enclosed within a wall. Although it looked good, the buildings didn't stand up well against the very occasional thunderstorms. Later, we were able to work up a convincing case to have the fort listed as a historical building (we included the fact that it had been the birthplace of Sheikh Zaid, the ruler of Abu Dhabi), so we got some extra money for its upkeep. After being shown around the fort, the sole British officer (the other one was on leave) briefed me on the squadron responsibilities and we had lunch together.

On leaving Buraimi, we didn't get far before it was time to make camp for the night. Once it was set up – cooking area shielded from the desert wind by a tent wall, night necessities unpacked etc. – a conversation ensued in broken Arabic, but here is the English version:

Mir: "Juma's wife and family live in Mahadha which we shall pass through tomorrow. He would like to stay there tonight."

Me: "Is it a long walk?"

Mir: "Yes, it is. He would like to take the Land Rover and be back here early tomorrow."

Me: "How early?"

Mir: "06.00."

Me: "Guaranteed?"

Mir: "Guaranteed."

Me: "Alright. But Juma, you mustn't drive fast."

Juma: "Thank you, sahib. And I'll see the Sheikh. He will invite you for coffee tomorrow."

Me: "No Juma. We can't have coffee with him. Mahadha is in Sultanate of Oman territory. We can pass through but mustn't stop except for operational reasons. But please give my salaams to the Sheikh."

That night there was no moon to compete with the stars. Out in the desert, looking up from my camp bed, I had never seen so many stars. Anyway, all worked out well. Juma had a night with his family and arrived back at the campsite just before 06.00.

Then on to Manama Camp, which was on the central gravel plain of the Trucial States. Two TOS squadrons were based there. It was training squadron's permanent base, and there was also a rifle squadron on its six-month rotation. In addition, the TOS Support Group (Machine Guns and Mortars) used it as a base when not out in support of one of the other squadrons. The training squadron had made itself quite comfortable over the years, unlike the rifle squadrons, which upped sticks every six months, leaving a bare utility camp of barusti (palm-leaf) huts and canvas marquees for the next occupants. On a later trip, I slept in one of the barusti huts.

They usually had a double palm-leaf roof which allowed air to circulate and generally kept them cool (well, sort of cool). Mosquito nets were essential! That particular night I heard someone creeping up on the gravel and prepared to meet the assailant. But the 'assailant', having found the door closed, made a fearful braying noise and pushed off. It was a wild donkey. There were usually several to be found near our camps.

Muaskar al Murqaab
(Watchtower Camp)

How do you like my new car?

This Identity Card is an official document issued by H.Q. Trucial Oman Scouts. Alterations are not permitted.

Authorising Officer _____

Date — 8 OCT 1968

TRUCIAL OMAN SCOUTS IDENTITY CARD No 2482

Number 4 6 1 1 8 5   Rank Captain

Name   D. J. T. DOWEY

Tribal Group Rebel

Thumbprint

CPU/66895/1.500/10.65

BURAIMI

Fort Jahili

2nd Lt Fahud Ali in his Buraimi compound with 2nd Lt Abdulrahman

Manama

Officers' Mess Sabre Squadron

Sabre Squadron Accommodation

MASAFI OUTPOST

DD at the Mess. (Note the stuffed parrot under the shade)

Masafi Camp

RAS AL KHAIMAH

Bedu

Shihuh Dancing
2nd Lt. Abdulrahman's Wedding.

The Hockey Team

Seven nationalities

Officers' Mess

Muaskar al Murqaab

Old TOS Mess

Sharjah

SHARJAH

Recruits, Day One.
Muaskar al Murqaab.

One day, the Recruits
will be on parade.

Pipes and Drums

DUBAI

The Creek

Dubai, Boat Building

Khor Fakkan

Mir Abdullah and Bank Guard

Beach Campsite

'The Fleet's in!'

Fishing - Circle complete so everyone heaves.
DD in the middle.

Dhows at anchor

Khor Fakkan from the jetty

Desert Travel with Mir

Near Masafi

Wadi-bashing on a good track

A Brew up

Mir copes with yet another puncture

Bedu
Moving camp

Desert well

Norton Barracks, Worcester.Final Parade of the Inniskilling Fusiliers (While I was in the Trucial Oman).

Camel Ride

Saddling up

Potential rider looking on anxiously

Al Him Ham

DD and JohnHutchings.at Al Him Ham on our Handover trip.

Al Him Ham. Early Days. Issa Mussa's Laundry.

Farewells for VIPs

My Farewell

John Hutchings, Tim Budd and Jeremy Bastin
make sure I catch the plane.

Colonel Pat Ive

The day of my induction visit to Manama coincided with the Scouts' Annual Rifle Meeting. The inter-squadron shooting was closely contested, but the finale had nothing to do with shooting. It had everything to do with camel racing. The inter-squadron race was bedlam. Far too many camels and riders milling around; nobody knew what was really going on. But the one for the Arab officers was terrific: a three-mile course tested the thoroughly competent riders on their racing camels. They lined up... well, they got in a sort of line. A shout sent them charging off. Away they went out into the desert, round a designated point and then they came hurtling back. The first three came in line abreast "Yahooing" for all they were worth. Really good. Then it was the British officers' turn. (I kept out of sight at the back, never having ridden a camel before.) To great shouts of encouragement and laughter, six or seven brave souls were helped onto their mounts, lined up and then they were away. Well, some went on their way, other mounts wandered around munching odd bits of vegetation while the furious riders tried to get them to move. Of those which actually galloped off, two didn't return. Search parties went out and eventually brought back the dishevelled riders and their nonchalant mounts. I suppose someone won but it was chaotic, with the troops laughing and roaring... the camels joining in the roaring, plus generally misbehaving.

From Manama, our route took us eastwards along a deep gorge up into the hills to Masafi; the highest of the TOS camps. The boundaries of several Trucial States met at or near the camp, and the squadron was often busy intervening in disputes of various sorts – boundaries, straying camels, blood feuds etc. Shots might be fired, the Scouts would intervene, everyone who was anyone would arrive amid much shouting and gesticulating. Then coffee would appear from somewhere and everyone would squat down. The Scouts would try to find a solution in which nobody lost any honour, and everyone would gradually drift away... until the next time. Sometime after my first visit to Masafi, I was back there staying overnight. X Squadron had moved in recently, Ken Wilson commanding. Ken was very Scottish and had his own way of speaking English. As I wandered around the small campsite before dinner, I came across a group of X Squadron soldiers; their corporal was giving them an informal English lesson.

"When Ingileez officer say you, 'Good morning', you are say, 'Good gracious'."

And he had them repeating that several times. It was typical Wilson-speak. The other memory of that visit was seeing the one item which departing squadrons did not steal and take with them – a cloth parrot on a perch on the Officers' Mess verandah! The famous Masafi Parrot. It remained there for good luck. Nobody would dare steal it!

The next leg of our trip took us north to the trucial state of Ras al Khaimah (RAK). A new camp would be required there shortly as Mirfa, down in Abu Dhabi, was to be handed over (hooray!) to British troops as a training camp. (The number of British troops in the Gulf had increased since the withdrawal from Aden.) RAK was a troublesome area, mainly due to the antics of a mountain tribe called the Shihuh. They had their own Arabic dialect and customs etc., and favoured the carrying of swords rather than guns. The Plains people thought of them as barbarians, but the Shihuh didn't care about that; as far as they were concerned, they were the top tribe in the Trucial States.

Then, on Day 7, we drove back to our base in Muaskar Al Murqab in Sharjah, having visited all of the squadron camps, passed through all seven of the Trucial States (plus part of the Oman) and covered around 700 miles. I now had some idea of the topography but also a fair idea of the conditions and problems that the squadrons had to face. Most importantly, I had a reasonable ability to prattle away in Jaysh Arabic. I didn't see much of the outgoing Staff Captain AQ (Admin and Quartering) due to his series of farewell social commitments among the expatriates of Dubai. While he was doing that, I settled down to 'read in' to the TOS regulations and files to help me understand how the Force operated.

Pat Ive, our colonel, had a lieutenant-colonel as his deputy. They were supported by a small Force HQ Staff (including me) and by HQ

Squadron. Also in the camp was one of the rifle squadrons. Rifle squadrons usually hated being at the HQ (although the officers liked the mess food) and couldn't wait to get back to the virtual independence of an outstation. Our communication with the outlying squadrons was via Morse signals, and the HQ Communications Centre was manned partly by Arab boy soldiers. When they weren't in class at our Boys' School or doing military training, those destined to be signallers manned the sets. Even the ones with rudimentary English did their turn, as the simple requirement was to recognise the individual letters of messages and send them in Morse – or to record each alphabet letter coming in and write it on a message pad. Most of the boys were extraordinarily fast at this and some of the senior boys were competent in English. On one occasion, a Royal Navy frigate was en route from Bahrain to Dubai to spend time on the coast in its anti-smuggling role. The ship signalled a challenge to us to play them at hockey. However, the RN signaller had obviously decided that he should send his Morse message very slowly in order to give the duty operator at this outlandish military force a chance to take down the message. No sooner had he finished his slow transmission than our 15-year-old Arab signaller shot back in English:

"Send message at normal speed or put competent operator on set!"

Alison stayed with her parents in York while I was away. The Le Tocqs were still living in St Peter's School accommodation – No.7 St Peter's Grove – but were in the process of buying No.12 – a few houses down at the bottom of the Grove. Alison was busy helping them to move, and also working for the York Minster Fund. This was an appeal to raise money for the restoration of certain parts of the Minster. She did manage a few days in Northern Ireland visiting my parents. Unsurprisingly, among other things, they took her to a Point-to-Point horse race meeting! Of course, many letters flew backwards and forwards between York and the Gulf and, every now and then, she would receive a large cardboard box from me. This probably seemed exciting to her at first, but apparently the anticipation gradually waned – the boxes usually contained old Arab coffee pots. The coffee pots weren't nice smart ones as sold in shops. Instead, Mir and I would wander round the artisans' quarter in Sharjah, exploring the workshops looking for discarded coffee pots which had been slung into obscure corners. Before they were packed for posting, Mir got to work cleaning them up. He found that putting them in a bucket of water and adding Army lemonade powder was great. (I abstained from Army lemonade powder after that!) Over the years, there have been clandestine attempts to 'lose' Arab coffee pots from our household. These attempts were unsuccessful for many years but gradually the memsahib got her way and now only a few can be seen somewhere in the house, though not prominently displayed.

Although we thought we were busy in Force HQ, the real work of the TOS was done by the five Sabre Squadrons:

A – Commanded by John Whitelaw, Queen's Own Highlanders

B – David Neild, King's Regiment

C – Rory Cochrane-Dyet, 16/5 Lancers

D – David Severn, Black Watch

X – Ken Wilson, Royal Scots

Each had a British 2I/C and three Arab subalterns. Apart from the normal ranks found in a British force, each squadron had a Matawa – a Moslem lay preacher. He had a particular standing among the soldiery and was usually well respected. Recruitment was generally good, except when the newly-formed Abu Dhabi Defence Force increased pay levels and a lot of our soldiers went west to join them! Then we had to increase our pay levels and quite a few drifted back to be with their mates. During the date harvest, soldiers were allowed away in relays to their villages, as long as the squadron strength did not drop below 80%. The desert tribesmen took some time to learn to be soldiers. They were amazed at the concept of discipline. Nevertheless, in time, many made good soldiers and were happy to serve in desert outposts, getting quite good money for their families and themselves… not forgetting the full bellies! Apart from the mainly desert-dwelling Bedu Arabs, we had Pakistanis, Indians, Baluchis,

Jordanians, Iranians, Dhofaris and Adenis plus a small smattering of other nationalities. The few Adenis were the last of the original troops which had been enlisted into the The Trucial Oman Levies – the original title of the Force when it was formed in 1951. With a few exceptions, the Adenis were unreliable and we were glad to see the back of them at the end of their engagements.

SC AQ and DAA&QMG. What does all that mean? Well, I had been posted in as the Staff Captain (Administration and Quartering). My immediate boss was the DAA&QMG (Deputy Assistant Administration & Quartermaster General); what a mouthful, but usually referred to as the DQ. When I arrived, the DQ was a major and reasonably efficient, though something of a bon viveur. He soon left, apparently because of the excessive heat of the Gulf. That meant I had to do his job, as well as mine, until his replacement arrived. I was very busy indeed. I can recall an occasion when five officers arrived in my office in quick succession and formed a sort of mob in front of my desk. Each claimed that they had a 'quick problem' which could be dealt with in a jiffy if I would only listen. Everyone scowled at everyone else. Blimey! Five of them with 'quick problems'. I threw my head back and laughed; they all joined in. Later, Desert Intelligence Officer, John Cousens of the Royal Artillery, who was nearing the end of his tour, was brought in for his last few weeks to help me. That did indeed help a lot. COMTOS asked MOD if he could retain me as DQ for the rest of my tour, but was told I was too young and too junior. Well, at least I got the pay of the higher rank. Very nice. During the working day I dealt with problems as they arose; in the afternoons and evenings, when the HQ was quiet, I addressed my in-tray. As acting DQ, I had one of the senior staff appointments in the Force. Al Qaid and his Deputy were supported by the senior operations staff officer Peter Rooke of the King's Own Scottish Borderers, the senior intelligence staff officer Tim Budd of the Royal Artillery and the DQ. So when the senior gang was invited somewhere, either for military or social reasons, I trotted along too. For example, we were invited to the ruler of Sharjah's residence for dinner.

On another occasion the five of us briefed the visiting Chief of the General Staff and had lunch with him.

My job included recruitment and discharge. There was a steady stream of applicants as riflemen, but many were turned away because of their age or due to medical reasons. Admin staff were also required at Force HQ. Emerging from my room in the mess at 05.30 each morning (we worked tropical hours for much of the year), I would sometimes find potential admin recruits squatting outside. These were mainly Pakistanis seeking work as clerks, storemen etc. Some proved to be very good, but many were chancers. The latter group usually used the dubious services of a well-known letter-writer who squatted under a large tree ('The Rola Tree') in Sharjah, where people seeking work would sit and wait for employment. Some would go to the letter-writer to get a CV which they would sign and bring up to our camp. The CVs had stock phrases, the most common being:

'I will leave no stone to be of your service, sir.'

A pity. '… no stone <u>unturned</u>…' might have got them an interview! At the end of job interviews, Mr Nair (our executive officer, a super chap from Kerala in India) would discuss the applicants with me. We would call back anyone we thought might be suitable and, after further questioning, would ask the crucial question, "Do you play hockey?" If the answer was yes, the potential recruit would be invited to attend that evening's hockey practice. If he was good, we recruited him without further ado. Mr Nair was fair but firm with staff. When I asked him if we ever had any complaints from military or civilian staff he said:

"If they complain, we sack them."

The system had always worked well. Everyone knew it, so who was I to change it?

One morning, as I approached my office, there was someone lying outside the door dozing. He heard me, leapt up, saluted and announced himself as a jundi (private) from D Squadron. What did he want? He wanted protection. He was involved in a blood feud arising from a Bedu desert

85

wedding. Soldiers were permitted to take their Army rifles to weddings. Practically all the Bedu carried rifles, some old rusted wrecks, but rifles nonetheless. But to have a smart British Army No. 4 Rifle was a sign of great pride on one side and envy on the other. TOS soldiers attending family weddings were issued five live rounds. The rounds were essential for the soldier's prestige so that he could fire off at the appropriate time in the wedding ceremony. Anyone who didn't have live ammunition was a nobody; TOS soldiers were certainly not nobodies. Anyway, this particular soldier had inadvertently left a round in the spout after the usual wild firing at a wedding ceremony. He cadged a lift home in the front of an open civilian Land Rover (ex-TOS vehicle beyond economical repair, of course). The back of the vehicle was crammed full of other returning soldiers. Our man was sitting in the front with the butt on the floor and barrel pointing towards the back. As the vehicle lurched over a bump, he inadvertently clutched the trigger and fired a shot. In the back, one dead TOS soldier! Never mind the military inquiry, it was blood-feud time. Our man haunted the HQ corridor (considered a safe haven) for some days and slept outside my office. Eventually, the blood price was agreed, paid, and he resumed his soldiering.

The TOS was funded equally by the MOD and the Foreign Office. Thus both the senior Army officer in Bahrain and the Political Resident (PR) there had some control over us. We didn't have much to do with the PR, however we worked closely with his political agents in Abu Dhabi and, mainly, in Dubai. The latter was frequently in our camp and sometimes invited the TOS officers down to his residence. We went there for a cocktail party on the Queen's birthday and took our pipes and drums with us. They were quite competent musicians, several of their senior ranks having attended the Army's Piping School in Scotland.

After Aden closed down, Land Forces Gulf (LFG) was set up in Bahrain under a Major-General. As acting DQ, I had reason to visit LFG from time to time. Bob Boulton had moved up with the staff from Aden. It was good to have an Inniskilling on the staff there to help introduce me around the HQ. And, of course, he and Patricia were very kind hosts. Patricia said that she liked to go to the fish market in Bahrain but wouldn't go by herself because of likely harassment. So instead, she would take one of her young sons; the Arabs made a great fuss of the little golden-haired boy, and she shopped happily and safely. At a cocktail party in the LFG Mess, I was talking to someone who I remembered from Berlin. He mentioned that one of the other staff officers had been Adjutant of the Anglians in Berlin. I remembered him and also his wife and described her as being blonde and vivacious, whereupon my friend said:

"She heard what you said. She's standing behind you!"

And she seemed to be very pleased with my description!

Gradually, LFG started to take more interest in what we did and sent messages and emissaries to tell us that we needed to conform more to British Army administration. Of course we resisted this, or simply ignored it. However, one thing that they did make us do was to get our drivers to complete vehicle work tickets. These recorded the journeys made by each vehicle showing timings, journeys, fuel etc. So we agreed. At the end of the first month we duly sent up all our vehicle work tickets to Bahrain for auditing and recording. They didn't ask for them again. The work tickets had been completed in Arabic!

It was no surprise to find 'characters' among the British officers in the Scouts. Most of the career officers on short tours of duty with the Scouts were, in the main, fairly normal. However, those who managed to get extended tours could be... well, a bit strange. In particular, the Desert Intelligence Officers. These chaps lived out in the wilds with a driver, an orderly, a radio set (maybe) and a Land Rover. Their title describes their job; they moved around and chatted, had a network of contacts and, periodically, reported back to base. We had one who had to be *ordered* back to base from time to time as he was inclined to go completely Bedu. A tall, thin chap with a beard, dressed in Bedu clothes and carrying a camel stick would arrive. A Bedu. Must be. *No, wait a minute ... it's Guy Gowlett!* We would keep him in camp for a week or so to debrief him. But, in particular, to make him a bit more like one of us again. You know... trousers, shirt, eat at table, speak English sometimes. Guy's boss was a real old denizen of the sands. Tim Budd was nominally a Royal Artillery officer but he had spent most of his military service with the Sudan Defence Force, the Singapore Forces and the Scouts. His knowledge of Arabic was good, his pronunciation dreadful. Strangely, the Arabs seemed to understand him. Anyway, he was a fixture and as people came and went, Tim stayed steady as a rock. A loyal Scout, very cheerful and widely respected.

Anyone who had anything to do with the TOS, including our visitors, knew Robbin Bastard. This old rogue of a silversmith, originally from Iran, had a workshop in a backstreet in Sharjah; he thoroughly deserved his nickname. His work was Professional, but he made a lot of money out of us and our visitors. A favourite memento of the Gulf was to have a 1780-dated Austrian Maria Theresa dollar (still used as currency in the Gulf in those days) incorporated into an ashtray. If you walk into any former TOS officer's living room you will very likely find one, or more, of them. Another favourite was a silver/pewter tankard engraved with the TOS badge. All produced by Robbin and each one made him a good profit.

Many people, both military and civilian, seemed to be fascinated by what they had heard about the Scouts and the Trucial States. In the cooler months, November to March, we had more visitors than we could really cope with. From April to October very few ventured down to see us; they knew about the heat and humidity. However, we did insist on some key players from Land Forces Gulf coming down during the foul weather months to see our working conditions, particularly in the outstations – the bulk of the Force – who worked through the summer without air-conditioning be they in their camps or, of course, out on patrols or operations. The most senior military visitor during my time was the CGS (Chief of the General Staff – you can't get much more senior than that!) Field Marshall Sir Geoffrey Baker, a charming man. We set up something to surprise him. Our Colonel (COMTOS – Commander TOS and his wife – COMTESSA) lived in a pleasant bungalow within our Sharjah camp and had staff to run the household and to organise hospitality. On Sir Geoffrey's programme was an informal lunch at the bungalow. He arrived by Land Rover. Those of us who would also be lunching gathered on the front steps. On hand was the Colonel's Senior Bearer, an ex-Indian Army soldier resplendent in turban, cummerbund etc. Leaving the Land Rover, Sir Geoffrey approached the steps... and suddenly stopped. Then he ran forward, as did the Bearer; they embraced with much happy shouting. The Bearer had been the General's orderly in the 4th Indian Division during World War Two. A lovely moment.

After the British pull-out from Aden in November 1967, more sophisticated military hardware started to appear in the Gulf. One example was the arrival of military helicopters. These had many uses, but one was to give military visitors a view of our area inside a day, whereas previously it would have taken several days to bump them around by vehicle. (Perhaps the latter was really the best way – to give them some idea of life in the TOS!) After I had accompanied one group of Bahrain military staff on an outstation tour by helicopter, I took them to dinner in Sharjah. A restaurant had been opened in what had previously been the Scouts' Officers' Mess. It was an imposing old building which overlooked Sharjah Creek. When the Scouts had it, they suffered from locals coming down to the creek edge at night and crapping – the Scouts did not appreciate the resulting smell drifting up to their verandah while they ate. Therefore, sometimes, before the evening meal was served, they would sit on the verandah in silence with the lights out. They would await a crapper, just let him crouch down, and then switch on all the verandah lights. The startled man would scuttle off to a hearty round of applause. He wouldn't be back and word would spread that crapping in front of the Scouts' Mess was not recommended.

In our new Sharjah HQ, the Officers' Mess kitchen received some basic daily rations and, in addition, officers received a daily ration allowance. We agreed to pay this into the messing fund. When I volunteered to be Messing Member at a mess meeting there was stunned silence – who on earth would volunteer for that? Well, I would. I wanted to eat well and, rather than complain about the efforts of others, I decided to give it a go. Each morning, after breakfast, I would meet with the duty cook. We had two cooks who took it turnabout each day. Both John and Younis were Pakistanis. They were great cooks… and hated the sight of each other. The first thing they would want to know in the morning was:

"What did *he* cook last night?"

Having considered the answer, they would leaf through Marguerite Patten's Cookbook to find something they could prepare for dinner. (I had asked Alison to send me out a well-illustrated cookery book, and Patten's was the one she sent. It was just the job.) Neither of the cooks could read English but, by looking at the coloured pictures, they could guess what was required. Then off to the one and only deep-freeze shop in Dubai to get the necessary ingredients. The implacable rivalry between the cooks ensured that we ate like fighting cocks. John had more service and was a corporal, but Younis was simply a jundy (a private). He fully deserved one stripe so I set him a task to earn it. First I asked Alison to send me the recipe (plus a photo) for one of her super puddings. We called it 'Gateau a la Hooch' (probably a kind of Gateau Diane). It was a meringue, chocolate and cream dish with some liquor added; very delicious. I read the recipe to him and we discussed the photo. Then, a severe warning that if his effort failed there would be no promotion. Of course, the results of his efforts were wonderful. Arise, Lance-Corporal Younis.

RAF cargo planes frequently did the round-trip – Bahrain-Sharjah-Masirah-Sharjah-Bahrain. (Masirah was an island just off the Oman coast in the Arabian Sea.) Prawns were plentiful and cheap in Bahrain, while crayfish were to be had in abundance off Masirah. So, after consulting the flight schedules, I would signal a friend in Bahrain or Masirah to request the necessary consignment. And then a return signal would arrive, saying something like:

"Done. Your consignment on afternoon flight Friday."

Occasionally things would go wrong with our order, such as it arriving on an earlier flight. When the driver went down to get them at the arranged time, he would be directed to a far corner of a hangar where a smelly box of long-gone-off seafood had been dumped. But when the system worked, the message would spread like magic and our dining room would fill with hungry TOS Officers; some even coming in from the outstations.

The cooks formed an uneasy alliance on 'Dinner Nights' (when we dined formally in uniform) when they realised that they had to work together or face the ire of the sahibs. We made sure that we praised them – equally – in glowing terms. One Dinner Night, having eaten, we were outside on the patio listening to three of the TOS pipers. Two of our officers (Englishmen) decided they had had enough of 'those wretched pipes' for one night and went off to collect a few thunderflashes. (These were very large firecrackers used on exercises to represent hand grenades – noisy but not dangerous when not too close.) Surreptitiously, they prepared a thunderflash for each of COMTOS and COMTESSA – no not the people, but the two miniature brass cannons which flanked the main door to the mess! Expertly, the thunderflashes were primed and dropped down the muzzles, followed quickly by two or three potatoes... and then... two mighty explosions. This was thought to be a good wheeze so yet more potatoes were fired. But we had forgotten something. The first sighting of the new moon was awaited up and down the Trucial Coast; it would herald the end of Ramadhan, and thus the end of the fasting period. The traditional way to signal that the holy men had glimpsed the new moon was the firing of cannons. Apparently, the little state of Ajman, just four miles away from our camp, heard our cannon fire and promptly followed suit with their cannons, and then others all along the coast did so too. But the new moon had not been spotted by the holy men – it wasn't seen until the next evening. Accusations raged up and down the coast about which state had falsely fired the first cannon and thus ended Ramadhan... and the fasting... one day early. We lay low!

The birth date of the Trucial Oman Levies, our predecessors, was March 19th, 1951. A parade was held on each anniversary. This took place at Muuaskar Al Muurqaab and the troops on parade consisted of the resident Sabre Squadron, HQ Squadron, the Drums and Pipes and the Horse Troop. Yes, we had a Horse Troop of around twelve horses. The riders were only part-time horsemen and had other jobs in the Scouts but, for big occasions, would mount up and swank around the parade ground with their lances. There would be a mixed gathering of guests. Usually the ruler of each of the Trucial States plus top British civilians like the Political Agent from Dubai. And all the flags of the states would be flying – all red and white but with variations of style. And for dinner that night we would have a special meal. On Scouts' Day in '68, when I was Messing Member, for the main course I provided each officer with his own roast chicken – a nice young pullet. That meant they couldn't crib about not being given their favourite part – a leg, a wing, the breast etc. At the next Mess Meeting, it was time to change some of the mess appointments; Wines Member and Food Member were to change. There were no volunteers to take on food so we looked around those present to see who wasn't there. Brian Gallagher of the Royal Ulster Rifles was on leave, so he was unanimously elected Food Member. And that's the way mess appointments were often made throughout the British Army. It was better to try to attend all mess meetings so that you could defend yourself and help nominate someone else for a mess job.

Dubai had changed quite a lot since I was first there in 1960. Even though it had found little oil yet, unlike Abu Dhabi further down the coast, Dubai benefitted from the spending power of Abu Dhabi. Also, it had free trade policies and just got on with it Dubai-fashion – it traded both legally and illegally. Much of the illegal trade was with India (Bombay in particular). One of the main trade items with Bombay was gold; India couldn't get enough of it. Even some of the TOS Officers were involved in this.

"If you, together with others, buy gold in Dubai and arrange for a dhow to take it for sale in Bombay, in the long term you will make quite a lot of money. Of course the Indian authorities sometimes catch a dhow and you could lose your investment but, if you keep at it, you will be fine. Around two dhows out of three get through. That's enough for you to make a good profit. Come on. You're Irish, and the Irish like a wee gamble."

But I didn't take my colleagues up on it.

At that time Dubai boasted one hotel. Well, there may have been doss-houses around but only one hotel, The Bustaan (The Garden). A few of us went there for an evening meal. It was fine but they were not well-stocked with wine.

"Do you have rosé?"

"I'll check."

"Sorry, no rosé. But I'll bring you a red and a white and you can make rosé for yourself." (Yes, that's an old one... but that's what he said!) Pretty good English, but pretty poor wine list.

But... wait a minute... what about my work? Was it all at the HQ? No. Every other weekend I'd set off in my Land Rover to visit a sabre squadron or two. The trip would include some sea-fishing, but much of the fun was wadi/hill/desert driving. Before a trip, I would give Mir the necessary money for the food. As cook for the trip he had the right of choice, which normally came down to tins of soup, bully beef (for currying), rice, onions, garlic, tinned fruit, biscuits, tea, coffee, sugar. He would stow that lot in a wooden box and have another box for his kitchen paraphernalia. As we set off on trips we would cry out:

"Bismillah!" (In the name of God!)

And:

"Seeda ila riml!" (Straight to the sands!)

Then we would take on our Bedu personae and chat, nonsensically, about our camels, sons, trouble with neighbouring tribes, weapons, etc. Our favourite quick meal was 'khubz wa liban'. Khubz was wafer-thin Arab bread up to two feet in diameter. Ours were made by Mir's wife. Liban was goat or camel milk; usually slightly curdled. Mir fried up garlic in ghee, poured on the liban and stirred the mixture. We would then tear up some khubz, roll it into a ball and dunk it in the liban. Right hand only. Lovely stuff. When possible, we would ask a Bedu to milk a camel for us so that we had fresh milk with our khubz. If we had no guest with us on our trip, Mir and I would sit around the campfire after supper and chat. I would be the top Sheikh of all the Bedu, with 4 wives, 20 children, many sheep, goats, camels, etc. Mir played the part of a simple hillman, and would ask me questions about all the various tribes… the Beni Kaan, Beni Kitab, etc. Good Arabic practice. On several occasions Chris Gee came with us. Chris was about my age and was the head of the MPBW (Ministry of Public Buildings and Works) in Sharjah. He lived in the RAF Sharjah camp and was delighted to get out on trips. Of course, he was a welcome visitor to our outstations; there was always something they wanted done. On one occasion we camped near Khor Fakkan, a village which belonged to Sharjah but which was over on the Arabian Sea coast. We hired a sailing dhow and had a lot of luck fishing. Later, we drove on up the coast to a picturesque little village called Bediyah. The men were down on the beach and, with the aid of a couple of boats, had laid a huge fishing net in a semi-circle from the beach. We helped them haul it in. Back-breaking work. Regrettably, all for nothing – they completely missed the shoal they were after. They weren't upset, it was Allah's will, so let's have some coffee. Chris and I often sang as we bucketed along in the Land Rover, much to Mir's disgust. He claimed that our singing brought on punctures. On one of our trips we covered Manama, Masafi, Buraimi and Abu Dhabi in two days. Four hundred miles of desert and wadi-bashing without a single puncture, thus puncturing Mir's theory. Back home at the end of a trip, off-load, and then Mir would raid my fridge for a tin of chopped mangoes. He would pound ice into mush, add the mangoes and we would have 'Mango Frappe'. Excellent. Towards the end of every trip, as we bucketed our way back to camp – tired, dusty and sweaty – we would be hallucinating about Mango Frappe.

With Mirfa closing, the Scouts needed a new squadron camp. The area chosen was a few miles south of Ras al Khaimah town. I went up with a surveyor and a building rep and set about marking the building outlines with lime dust. Once the building programme was under way, there were many more trips. And eventually it was ready for B Squadron to move in. A couple of days later I received a signal from the two British officers. They were apparently trying to paint the walls inside their tiny mess.

"We've tried every known proportional mix of green and yellow but can't get an acceptable blue. What should we do?"

Well, what could you expect from Infantry officers in, respectively, the King's Regiment (David Neild) and the Queen's Regiment (Nigel Harris) both of whom were drinking beer while they tried to get the right mix of paint? Both must have failed Art at school.

There were two main ways to Buraimi (now Al Ayn) from Sharjah: the desert route, and the mountain route. We favoured the 'mountain route' which was rather a misnomer but a useful short and snappy name; you headed across part of the desert towards the mountains, and then used various mountain wadis to continue, thus missing much of the open desert. Occasionally the Trucial States were subjected to thunderstorms. When that happened, the vehicle tracks in the desert were wiped out and you had to find your own way through. But even if the tracks had been wiped out, you had one very useful marker as you left Sharjah – a lone acacia tree just a few miles out in the desert. This poor tree had been hit by several vehicles over the years, even though it was the only tree for hundreds of yards around. Drivers knew to head for it as a firm marker to help them on their way. As they approached, they could well be chatting to others in the vehicle and not concentrating… when all of a sudden… smack…. straight into the poor tree. There were odd bits of metal lying around it.

On one occasion driving to Buraimi, this time using the desert route, we came across an elderly Bedu trekking along leading a camel.

Us: "As-salaamu alaikum."

"Haya kulla!" That was him.

After a few minutes of his guttural chat, during which we refilled his chaggals (goatskin water carriers) from our water jerrycans, we moved on.

"What was he talking about, Mir? I could hardly understand a word he said."

Mir explained that he was an old Bedu with a strong tribal dialect. 'Haya kulla' was his way of saying 'Wa alaikumu as-salaamu'. Apparently, the old man went on to complain that all the young Bedu were heading for the towns to get jobs so desert-living was coming to an end.

On another trip to Buraimi, we left Sharjah one afternoon and camped for the night near the track. By this time we had already suffered two punctures! Well, that didn't worry us unduly as we always carried two spares. However, the next morning during our 'first parade inspection' (oil, petrol, water, tyres) we discovered... another flat tyre! Consultation with Mir, who explained that there was a Sultan's Forces Gendarmerie post over towards the mountains about five or six miles away. They could come out with a spare tyre and later mend our punctures. So I jogged off down the track. The long and the short of it was that the Gendarmerie rescued us with a spare tyre, repaired our tyres and sent us on our way.

"Thanks very much. Call in to see us in Sharjah if you are passing. Fee amaan Illah!"

"Fee amaan al Kareem!"

Yes, the Bedu brought their traditional hospitality with them into the Security Forces.

We hadn't been to Buraimi for a couple of months, but even in that short time it had changed. Sheikh Zaid, the ruler of Abu Dhabi, had money rolling in from the oilfields. Where only months before there had been just sand dunes, roads were now being built including one from Buraimi down to the coast, to Abu Dhabi town itself. Zaid had been born in the fort at Buraimi and, for a while, had considered having his capital there. That could have been a good idea; it was much less humid in summer than Abu Dhabi town on the coast.

At that time, one of the few ways in which the poorer Trucial States could gain some foreign currency was to produce stamps. A continual stream appeared with amazing subject matters; who would have thought that one of the states would produce a set of stamps depicting many of the Winter Olympic sports? Well it did, and many other bizarre events and activities adorned further issues. Alison was a stamp collector so I would get first day covers and send them off to her. They are probably still in a box somewhere – and still worthless! Anyway, it was time for a stamp-collecting safari. Cpl Bill Thitchener, one of the NCOs in the HQ, was a philatelist and he jumped at the chance to come with Mir and me on a weekend trip. Besides visiting TOS outposts, we went round the poorest states (Ajman, Umm al Qawain, Fujairah and Ras al Khaimah) hunting out the 'Post Offices' and buying stamps. Thitchener was keen to get a certain 'first-day-issue' from the previous year. This proved to be no problem to one of the postmasters. He simply span the dial on his stamping machine to the appropriate date, bonked the stamps and, *voila*, there was a first-day envelope. However, our trip was not well-timed. There were continual thundershowers and we bogged down several times and had two tyre blow-outs (*we now carried three spares*). Also, we had to hurriedly seek higher ground for a while when the wadi we were in started to flow with water from a downpour up in the mountains. (We heard later that Tim Courtenay, a Royal Marine officer who was 2I/C of one of the squadrons, had had serious problems in another wadi that day. He had to use his Land Rover's tow-chain to anchor the vehicle to a rock, then sat on the side of the wadi for two hours, waiting for the torrent to subside.) It was teeming with rain when we got to Khor Fakkan (an enclave of Sharjah) on the Arabian Sea, so camping out without a tent was not an option. We asked in a shop where we could stay for the night.

"Stanna shwaya." (Wait a moment.)

A lad was despatched and returned a few minutes later with the Chief of Police.

"How can I help you?" said the Chief.

Very soon we were guided to the Sheikh of Sharjah's guesthouse. All modern conveniences.

"Be our guest," said the Chief.

Were the Arabs hospitable? Oh yes, indeed they were.

In the TOS we had our own Navy. Well, that's not strictly true; we had a motorised dhow called '*Al Qaid*' (The Commander). The idea was that it could patrol the coast looking for pirates, slave-traders and smugglers. The trouble was that those people had dhows with very powerful engines; they could usually outrun Al Qaid. Anyway, we were allowed to hire the dhow plus crew if it was not otherwise engaged. A party of TOS officers and their guests would usually board it in Dubai creek, carrying picnic and drinks boxes and probably accompanied by a waiter from the mess to help. Off we would go for a trip up the coast, a swim off a sandy beach (not hard to find) and some fishing. Once, when the dhow was based for a while at Ras al Khaimah (RAK), we drove up and boarded her there. The RAK scenery was much more interesting than Dubai/Sharjah. RAK is backed by rugged mountains and further northwards along the coast there were several fishing villages. While we sailed along, drinking and chatting, a Royal Navy minesweeper hove into view. When she came closer we could see that she was *HMS Appleton*.

"Come aboard!" we shouted. "Help us with our picnic."

But by now they had noticed that we had a very beautiful young lady with us (the daughter of a senior officer based in Bahrain).

"No, it's better that you come on board the *Appleton*. We'll send a boat across."

So all eight or so of us ended up in their tiny wardroom, drinking champagne with their officers. Very cramped indeed. But that, I'm sure, was the dastardly naval plan: to get as close as possible to our lovely young lady.

"We'd better be going. We've a long sail on a slow boat."

"No, no, make a night of it. All of you can stay with us," they said as they continued to eye up our young lady.

"No, not possible, old chap. We Pongos must get back to our duties. With our precious cargo."

So we escaped from the grasping clutches of the Royal Navy… with our lovely young lady.

From time to time, Al Qaid devised a Force Exercise to involve all squadrons (less one troop each which remained at their base camps to deal with emergencies). Mir, plus a driver and a signaller (both strangers to me), and I climbed into my Land Rover and set off with all our gear and a complete set of exercise instructions; we were umpires. This was in May and it was very hot already, but the soldiers were pretty cheerful. It was Ramadhan time – the month of fasting – and if they had remained in camp, they would have had to observe strict fasting rules. On exercise they were exempt from fasting. And most of them seemed to enjoy exercises and really entered into the spirit of it all. I was impressed with their fitness as they doubled along through the sand and raced up hillsides, yelling their heads off just for the sake of it.

For the next phase of the exercise we took a shortcut over the sand dunes. The Land Rover laboured up the dunes and slid down the other side. Then we climbed a particularly high dune, went over the top and slid very quickly to the bottom. Problem. We were now at the bottom of a huge hollow with steep sides all round.

"Try the radio to see if you can contact any of the other vehicles."

"Hallo all stations. This is Umpire 3. Can you hear me?"

He tried a few more times, but our signals were not clearing the high dunes.

Blimey! Will we ever get out of here? It would be very difficult to haul the heavy radio set up the sandy sides, and even then we might not be able to make contact as the exercise would have moved on. We'll have to drive out. So the four of us went slipping and sliding up the sides, and out on to the desert gathering the sparse bush growth and tumbling it down to the bottom. Fortunately, we carried two metal sheets lashed to the side of the Land Rover for such a contingency and now we had the bushes to give some extra traction to the wheels. So began a long and arduous episode of laying down the metal sheets and bushes, advancing a few feet, then recovering them and doing the same thing again. Again and again under a blazing sun with no breeze. We made progress slowly, going up spirally.

After some four or five hours, at last we reached the top. Exhausted. All of our water had been drunk.

"Hallo all stations. This is Umpire 3. Can you hear me?"

Well, they could, and we eventually made rendezvous with Al Quaid.

"Derek! Where the devil have you been? I didn't think you Infantrymen ever got lost!" (He was a Cavalryman.)

"Ah well, Colonel, let's just say we had an adventure and learnt a lot about getting a vehicle out of a sand trap… and we learnt a lot about ourselves for that matter."

(I think of that episode when faced with a major problem. Surely if I could get out of that scrape I can deal with most things?)

Trips away from camp, hockey, and runs down to the beach were my main leisure pursuits to make breaks from my very busy job. A typical day in camp from April to October (the hottest months) would go something like this:

05.30	Office
09.00-09.45	Breakfast. Enormous. (Indian Army style)
13.30-15.30	Rest. (No lunch)
15.30-19.00	Office (tea and sandwiches around 16.30, courtesy of Mir)
19.30	Dinner
21.30	Bed

I rarely had lunch but ate like a horse at breakfast and dinner. In the delightful winter months we would start later and work through the afternoons. One evening I drove to Ajman Creek, about four miles away. There was a large natural lagoon which gave protection to the small fishing fleet. The sandy beach sloped steeply into the lagoon, and I sat there idly throwing pebbles into the water. A fin broke the calm about fifty meters offshore. A dolphin. It circled around for a while and then disappeared. Suddenly it appeared in front of me and thrust its upper body onto the beach. We looked at each other from a distance of a yard or so. Then, with a flick, it turned and went out again to swim in lazy circles.

Presumably it had sensed the splashes of my pebbles or seen the ripples and had come to investigate. Amazing.

Our weekend was Friday and Saturday; Friday being the Moslem holy day. We did well for holy days and were free (technically) from work on important days in both the Christian and Moslem calendars – Christmas, Easter, New Year, End of Ramadhan, Celebration of the Sacrifice etc. That suited most people. Some took the days off, some caught up with their work. St Patrick's Day 1968 fell on a Sunday – neither a Force holiday or weekend. But Colour Sergeant McKenzie of the Irish Guards took the day off anyway. He set himself up on the verandah outside his room in the Sergeants' Mess with a case or two of Guinness and several bottles of Irish whiskey. Comfortable chairs were added to his shebeen and he took on all comers throughout the day and into the evening.

"Come on now. Sit yourselves down. Now, what would you be wanting, Sir? A drop of the Cratur (*meaning whiskey*) or some Liffey Water *(meaning Guinness)*. What will it be?"

And then, of course, he attended the Sergeants' Mess party that evening to which the officers were invited. He was still in great form when I spoke to him:

"Colour, thanks for your hospitality earlier but you celebrated on the wrong day."

"I most certainly did not! This is the 17th – Saint Patrick's Day! And you of all people should know that!"

"Well, today's Sunday, and so in Ireland they're taking the day off work tomorrow, Monday. That's when they'll celebrate Saint Patrick in style."

"You're pulling my leg, Sir!"

"No. That's what happens when the Saint's day falls on a Sunday. The Monday is the National Holiday in Ireland and that's the day for celebration."

"Holy Jayzus! I should have been celebrating tomorrow!"

"Yes, you should. I suggest you go and see Al Qaid and explain that you need the 18th off as well. Tell him you made a tragic mistake over dates.

101

Otherwise the whole of Ireland will be celebrating in style tomorrow while you will be in the stores counting boots and things."

He went off looking for Al Qaid muttering, "Tragic mistake."

D Squadron was in residence at the HQ barracks in Sharjah when Louis Wilkes, their 2IC, mentioned that one of his soldiers was getting married out in the sands east of Dubai. Would I like to come along? Certainly I would. So a gang of us set off in three Land Rovers and a 3-tonner; the men were dressed up in their best civilian finery... white, flowing robes but with red/white warrior shemagh headdress. We were heading for a small oasis about 15 miles out in the sands. Someone knew where it was and we stopped in sight but about two hundred yards away. This was normal routine. The men debussed and formed a line abreast before advancing and firing off their five rounds per man (normal allocation for a TOS wedding). The sweating groom came running out to meet us. He seemed to be doing everything without a 'best man' in sight. Proceedings started with the squadron Matawa (lay preacher) reciting a short prayer. Then we had sweet food – halva, fruit and sweet noodles. Plus, of course, coffee. This was just the appetiser. Soon, the cooked food appeared and we all squatted down around trays heaped with rice and steaming mutton. Right hand only, don't show the soles of your feet/shoes. In the background, young Arab girls with long greased hair were standing in line and leaning forward, swinging their long hair back and forth to the beat of drums. Very traditional apparently, but after a minute or so not much to watch. However, our soldiers were entranced by it. With the food finished, it was time for the men (only the men) to dance. They trooped around in a wide circle, dancing to the rhythm of drums and swinging their rifles. Some of them could twist, throw, spin and catch their rifles with amazing dexterity. At the back of the tents, set up for the occasion, the women peeped out. Of course, the men were showing off like mad. Then came the camel racing. They were real racing camels – sprinters. Many of the soldiers took their turn in two-camel duels. They would trot down to the start, about four hundred yards away, and come galloping back, roaring and shouting and whacking their camels while everyone else yelled. I wasn't allowed a solo performance but did get on behind one of the riders. Once we really got going it was a smooth ride. Some wedding celebrations can last a week, but we (Louis and I) had to get back for a Dinner Night in the mess.

Sometime later I was invited to 2Lt Abdulrahman Rahman's wedding, up in Ras al Khaimah territory. A few days before the event I was chatting with him. He said he had been browned off for weeks about the prospect of the wedding (his English was rather good). He was very critical of his people's tradition regarding arranged marriages.

"It's ridiculous for me to have to marry a girl I have seen only once. That was years ago when she was a schoolgirl. And my father is spending £5000 on a wedding I don't want – £1600 to the bride, £2000 for our house, some to the father of the bride, the rest on the wedding itself. The whole thing is crazy."

However, it was a fine wedding and it was good to see Abdulrahman relaxed and smiling, and obviously enjoying himself. The men's dancing was different to that of the desert tribes. This was Shihuh country and the Shihuh tribesmen preferred swords to rifles. They were all charging around swinging their swords in mock battle. The spectators stood well back.

One of my ex-officio jobs was Locust Control Officer for the Trucial States. Pardon? Yes, that's right. My induction into the job was pretty quick and simple. During handover, my predecessor drove me to an open area just outside Sharjah town. We stopped beside a small fenced-off area about ten yards square. Well, most of the fence was lying on the ground, and there were ample signs that goats used the area a lot. The 'equipment' consisted of half a dozen sacks of pesticide. Most of the sacks were split and their contents had dribbled out. That was it.

"So what do I do with this lot?"

"Well, if there is a plague of locusts, you round up a few soldiers and shovels, come down here, load up with the pesticide and go out and chuck the stuff at them."

Or words to that effect.

"And there is some sort of Pakistani civilian Locust Control Section which, if you ever see them, you may want to liaise with. Oh yes, there's a file somewhere in the office with the contact details for the central Locust Control Office in London. If you think you need more insectide you should contact them."

I got a new consignment of sacks of pesticide and kept them in our camp. Some weeks later, Rory Cochrane-Dyet (9th/12th Lancers) OC C Squadron, signalled me from Masafi.

"My dog has caught a thing like a locust. It has lost its head but the rest is intact. What shall I do with it?"

Later that day a driver appeared in my office clutching an envelope marked 'Headless Fred'. Inside was indeed a headless locust. I signalled Locust Control in London, and the radio waves became very busy:

"Where found exactly?"

"Any others found?"

"Vegetation showing signs of chewing?"

"When last rainfall?"

"Where?"

"Please tell troops to report sightings immediately." etc.

Fred was duly hung on my wall in a bottle of formalin for recognition training whenever anyone visited my office. Ten days later... another envelope... this time marked 'Esmeralda'. It had been found in Sharjah. This really got the London Office hopping. (*Nice one that... locusts... hopping? Oh well.*) And a week later an envelope arrived from John Whitelaw, the Highland officer commanding A Squadron in Manama, 'Egbert the Timorous Wee Beastie'. What?! A third one? Almost a plague of locusts! More panic in London. But fortunately, no more locusts were reported in my time in the Trucial States.

After we abandoned the dreaded camp at Mirfa, it was set up as a desert training centre for British Troops stationed in Bahrain, so we started to see more of them. Companies would come down from Bahrain for training and a battalion was based in the RAF camp in Sharjah. Our Arab soldiers couldn't understand the purpose of the troops. After all, the TOS were here and had proved for years that we could handle any situation that arose.

"They can't move quickly, sahib. Say there was a problem at Buraimi which our squadron there couldn't handle. The Sharjah Squadron could be there within five hours. The British would take up to two days as they don't understand desert driving."

The TOS soldiers didn't show much interest in sport apart from a type of wild soccer and, on occasion, camel racing. However, there were usually enough competent hockey players in HQ jobs in Sharjah to field a reasonable team. We had an interesting mixture of skills and wildness among the English, Irish, Welsh, Scotch, Pakistani, Indian and Persian elements of the Force HQ hockey team (but no Bedu). A challenge was received from the oil people on Das Island, just off the coast of Abu Dhabi. So we bounced our way down to Abu Dhabi in trucks, and then boarded a Dakota for the short flight to Das. It had been a remote, uninhabited, rocky island… and then offshore oil was discovered nearby. Its landscape changed forever when it was chosen to be the supply base for the Umm Shaif oilfield. A harbour, an airstrip, housing and a hospital were constructed. On this former desert island, our hockey team was entertained royally in their 'Counties Pub' which displayed a shield for every county in the United Kingdom. In front of the pub stood the stocks… for those who misbehaved in the pub. Their terrific hospitality was an obvious ploy to try to wreck our chances in the hockey match on the morrow. When we took to the field the next day I didn't recognise any of the opposition, not because I was suffering from the night before, but because we suspected that their hockey players had sneaked off to bed for a good night's sleep before the party got really going. However, their evil plans (which we had enjoyed thoroughly) came to nothing as we just managed to beat Das 2-1. They couldn't believe it as they usually trounced visiting teams. A return match was demanded. We accepted the challenge. A month or so later they flew up to Sharjah seeking revenge. Of course, we employed the same 'evening before' tactics that they had tried on us. We were wholly successful in this... gave them a great time... and then thrashed them 8-0 the next day!

In November 1967, the Wilson/Falkender government had issued an assurance to the Sheikhs of the Trucial States that the British military presence would be maintained in the Gulf region. The Sheikhs were relieved to hear this. They had, for years, felt the threat of Saudi Arabia who would love to get their hands on the oil in their region. (They also kept a very close eye on Iran). Then, in January 1968, the bombshell. The Wilson/Falkender government announced that, apart from keeping forces in Hong Kong, the British military presence east of Suez would be withdrawn by the end of 1971. This meant that our military forces would return from Singapore and Malaysia, and from the Gulf and from other smaller enclaves. This had a shattering effect on the Gulf rulers; two months previously they had been assured that the British military would remain in the Gulf. Perfidious Albion. They were now looking in all directions to see where they could run for cover. The announcement also had a shattering effect on me, the globetrotter. At the age of 28, and with the Staff exam coming up in the next couple of years, many excellent overseas postings were about to disappear and, more importantly, the Army would be reduced in size. This included my own Regiment, the Inniskillings, who were to be amalgamated with the other two Northern Irish Infantry regiments – the Ulster Rifles and the Irish Fusiliers. So what should I do? The Regiment I had been born into, my Regiment, was disappearing. East of Suez postings were being cut back and the Army was getting smaller. Well, I gave much thought to the problem and decided I needed a trade (perhaps flying or finance) as infantry officers aren't usually in high demand in civilian life. Transfer within the British Army or perhaps try for the Australian Army? Then, at the due time, I could become a civilian with something to offer. Alison and my parents were shocked. Also, Alison came under pressure from her parents to dissuade me. Anyway, I was due leave, and went back to the UK. We had a lovely time together in York, Guernsey and Belfast. By the end of the leave I could see that the idea was definitely not a happy one in the family circle.

"You've done pretty well in the infantry and now you're going to throw that away!"

When I got back to the TOS, I withdrew my resignation. The problem then arose that my two replacements had been nominated – Jeremy Bastin of the 15th/19th Hussars as Staff Captain AQ and John Hutchings of the Royal Anglians as DAA&QMG. Colonel Pat Ive had asked MOD to let me stay as DAA&QMG for my full tour in the TOS but they wouldn't allow that. Too junior.

A little while later, I was told I would be posted to HQ 6 Infantry Brigade as Intelligence Officer. But not only Intelligence – also Security, Nuclear, Biological and Chemical warfare. That would mean attending a course at the Intelligence Corps HQ in Ashford, Kent. Oh, and 6 Brigade HQ was in Barnard Castle up in County Durham. From the heat and sands of the Trucial States to the snow and sleet of Durham in January 1969. So my TOS story is almost finished, but events could have taken a different course if I had taken up Issa Mussa's offer.

Issa Mussa? His name translates as Jesus Moses – not uncommon among Moslems. He was the contractor to the TOS (as he was to the fledgling military forces in some of the other Gulf States); a clever, likeable rogue. A Persian who was barely literate, he had worked himself up from being a camp sweeper on the Sharjah airfield during World War 2, to being one of the richest men in the Trucial States. Issa provided canteens, laundries, tailors' shops, etc. to the military forces. Our new camp at Ham Ham in Ras al Khaima was beginning to take shape and Issa asked if he could go up with me when I next visited. He wanted to see the area allocated to him. So that was arranged. On the way up, he told me that he had heard that I would be leaving the Scouts shortly; he asked if I would like to stay on in the Trucial States and work for him as his British frontman. This caught me by surprise. I thanked him for his generous offer but told him that my immediate future had already been decided. So here was another point in my life where there was more than one path available to follow. Perhaps it was just as well that I did not take up the offer, as four years later I heard that Issa had died. Whoever took over his enterprises may not have wanted me as his British frontman.

My departure date was fast approaching and my relief (well, my two reliefs) had arrived, but there was one major thing I had still to do – ride a camel solo. What?! A TOS man who had never ridden a camel! Mir, my orderly, arranged to put that right. Chris Gee from MPBW said he would like to join in, as did Jeremy Bastin who had just arrived and was to be the new Staff Captain. We drove out of camp to a prearranged spot to meet a camel man. He had the necessary camels and immediately he and Mir got stuck into heated bargaining – furious shouting and waving of arms. Eventually, money changed hands and, after some difficulties (like mounting the camels), we set off for the beaches beyond Ajman. Mir drove on ahead in the Land Rover with his cooking boxes, and by the time we reached the beach he had a feast ready for us. We needed it. The camel ride had been hard work; there didn't seem to be much rhythm to a camel's progress as we lurched along on top of them. Even cavalryman Jeremy looked like an unsteady sack of potatoes. I fell off – much to the joy of the other two who declared I had failed my driving test. But I could still say I had ridden a camel – in the desert! Indeed camels were still being used by TOS patrols, particularly down in the Liwa Oasis area, near the border with Saudi Arabia. Even the Dodge trucks with 'balloon' tyres had difficulty with some of the terrain, and camels were used instead.

As my time for leaving approached, I visited each of the outstations to say farewell. I managed to hitch a flight down to Buraimi in a Beaver airplane. A recently commissioned Arab officer, Fahud Ali, accompanied me round some of the villages and, as we went along, we were hailed by soldiers on leave. They shouted:

"Come to my barusti. Tafdl, tafdl!"

A barusti was a palm hut, and 'tafdl' meant eat/drink. And we would have to go in and have coffee, dates and other fruit. Then we stopped at Fahud Ali's barusti.

"Now we eat properly."

"No, no. I'm full after all that coffee and fruit."

A feast had been prepared by his wife.

"Eat! Or by God I shall be offended!"

I ate.

Back to Sharjah by Land Rover via Abu Dhabi (unfortunately the plane had other things to do). Sheikh Zaid had been busy with road improvements so we made good time. But it was boring driving in a straight line on a good surface. The adventure of driving through desert and mountain in the Trucial States was fast becoming a thing of the past.

The night before an officer was to leave the Scouts (and there were many departures because of the short one/two-year tours) he would have a private party in the mess. He would consult with the duty cook about the menu, and part of the anteroom and dining room would be partitioned off for him and his guests. He would leave the next day. Scouts' farewells to the top men (COMTOS, D/COMTOS or RSM) entailed being towed through the camp and out of the gate (many hands on many ropes towing a Land Rover), preceded by the Pipes and Drums, and with everyone else lining the route and shouting nice things (hopefully). Other farewells were much less formal. The departing individual (often still inebriated from the night before) would be taken in a convoy of Land Rovers to RAF Sharjah. The airport would then be virtually taken over by the farewell mob (the duty RAF Flight Lieutenant would stay quietly out of the way). The well-wishers would be standing on Land Rovers and toasting the departing one with champagne (and making sure he had some too); there would be much shouting and perhaps some singing. A more senior RAF officer might appear on the scene but, because he would quickly realise that there wasn't much he could do, would either disappear or join in. In the event of a mechanical breakdown and no take-off, the whole procedure would have to be repeated the next day – by which time the departing one would have an ashen pallor about him. My day came and it was sad to leave my friends and my Baluch orderly, Mir Abdullah. Mir had looked after me well and was always respectful and indeed, a good friend. He gave me a wicked-looking Baluchi knife which he claimed was around fifty years old – so that makes it a centenarian now. But, no matter. I was on my way to be with my lovely wife, Alison.

I was no longer an Inniskilling. The Royal Inniskilling Fusiliers (the 27th Regiment) with 279 years of service had just been amalgamated with the other two Northern Irish regiments – the Royal Ulster Rifles (the 83rd Regiment) and the Royal Irish Fusiliers (the 86th Regiment). We became the Royal Irish Rangers.

How had my time been in the Trucial Oman Scouts? What can I say other than – *What an Adventure!*

Farewell to the Sands

Made in the USA
Monee, IL
17 December 2022

19182938R00066